WHEN GOOD WAITERS DO BAD THINGS

A MEMOIR

by

K.L. LAYTIN, Ph.D.

When Good Waiters Do Bad Things

This book is a memoir, not a history book or an autobiography. I have tried to recreate events, locales and conversations from my memories of them. I have changed the names of places and some identifying characteristics and details. Names have been changed to avoid hurting anyone and to protect the innocent, although as you read this memoir, you will note that it is hard to find anyone who was truly innocent.

ISBN-13:

978-0692084984 (K. L. Laytin, Ph.D.)

ISBN-10:

0692084983

Printed in the United States of America

This book is dedicated to my late, beloved grandfather, Abe Rifkin, who refused to ever tip a waiter. His logic was straightforward. "I'm paying for the food. Do they expect me to go into the kitchen and get it myself?" Later in life, he became a very generous tipper and insisted others around be generous as well, after his eldest grandchild began working summers as a waiter.

ACKNOWLEDGEMENTS

Sincere thanks to a number of people, including several family members and some good friends for their encouragement, valuable suggestions and proofreading as I wrote this memoir. They include my loving wife, Rose Laytin, my mother, Jeanne Laytin as well as Thomas Maher, Wayne Laytin, Dr. Dennis W. Kogut, Robert W. Galvin, Judy Fosdick, Renée Cohen, Lydia Hart and Allen Mogol.

TABLE OF CONTENTS

Teitelman's Inn

1
TEITELMAN'S INN

It was a picture postcard New England winter day in rural Connecticut on December 23, 1965. Light flakes were in the air as we drove past white, wood-framed farm houses that went on for miles and miles. The air was cold and crisp and a thin layer of snow had settled on the ground. What the postcard could not have shown was that the air carried a strong smell of manure as we approached the only hotel of its kind, a strictly kosher hotel in the middle of Connecticut's dairy cow and egg farm country.

The hotel was located a few miles from the center of Kirby, a little town known only to a select few outsiders, all of whom have advanced degrees in American Colonial History. It seems that George Washington did something noteworthy there one night in 1778, in a building built just outside of town in 1742 and used by Connecticut Governor Jonathan Trumbull during the American Revolution. Unclear was whether the town was on the map because of what Washington did there or because the building he did it in was still standing. In any event, traveling just a few hours to Kirby, Connecticut gave me a real sense of how unlike the Bronx, Connecticut was. Farm houses, cow barns, an Amoco station, chicken coops and a package store were all that I saw for the last

10 miles. Some of the houses looked as though they dated from Washington's time, with two stories of white clapboard and large center chimneys. While some of the houses were lovely, the passage of time had stolen the structural symmetry from others, unless one considers parallelograms to have symmetry. Oddly, the names on the signs and mailboxes of the dairy farms were almost all 12 or 13 letters long, with unpronounceable sequences of consonants often starting with "scz." This was not where I expected to find a kosher hotel. Compared to where I lived in the Bronx, however, the area was beautiful, if you could get past the smell and liked places this rural. I was to work as a busboy at the hotel for the Christmas through New Year's holiday.

My Uncle Phil had made the job arrangements. He and my aunt lived in a town about 18 miles from the hotel and he had been a waiter there a generation earlier under its previous owners. My uncle was now an insurance salesman doing business with the hotel's current owners, Morris and Edna Teitelman, or Mr. and Mrs. T., as they were known. He told me that while Mr. and Mrs. T. continued to buy insurance through him, they made him kick back a cut of his commission to them as a condition of giving him their business. In return, the Teitelmans let my cousins use the swimming pool during the summer. Not a good deal for my uncle, as was evident on his face as he told me in confidence about the arrangement. Knowing that, plus the fact that this was a hotel serving kosher dinners for the Christmas holiday in the land of Connecticut Yankees, immigrant farmers and hen houses, made me suspicious, but the prospect of making a lot of money as a busboy was a strong motivator. And I only had to do it for ten days. I could handle that.

Approaching the hotel, a large, three-story, wood-frame building set right along the road came into view, with its painted Teitelman's Inn sign. We were here. The white clapboard of the building, the snow and large, leafless trees, all said winter in New England. From its small "welcome" sign out front, it appeared we had stopped at the hotel's main building. The side of the building looked across the country road at a narrow, frozen lake. There was a small sandy beach along the lake, mostly covered with snow. The lake was long enough that you could barely see the other end. A sign said "Lake Gilmer." I could see other buildings on the hotel grounds including some probably from the 1920's or 1930's and several more modern buildings, probably from the 1950's. The place had a bit of character with broad, snow covered, rolling lawns and large snow-whitened oak and maple trees standing everywhere. Snow-covered benches were scattered along the walkways and under trees.

I assumed the other large wooden buildings to be guest residences. A smaller but more modern colonial-style home looked down majestically from upon a hill in the distance. One of the guest buildings had tall white columns supporting its front porch. Another had an endless porch around it. In many ways it was lovely, very winter in New England, except that some of the buildings were interconnected through giant, enclosed, above-ground green plastic tubes. Hamster Habitats come to mind, designed for giant, mutant hamsters. Their purpose had to be for hotel guests to travel between buildings without having to go out into the weather, but they detracted severely from the place's New England character. It was two days before Christmas, 1965. I was 16. My parents had driven me the 105 miles from the Bronx to the hotel. Although I owned a 1955 Buick Super Convertible, you had to be 18 to drive legally in New York City. You could drive outside of the city at 16 during the day but could not drive unsupervised in New York State after dark. At 16, with my limited New York license, I was not allowed to drive at all in Connecticut. The legality of my early driving aside (it never had stopped me before), I had purchased my Buick for $15 and its ability to make the 210 mile round trip was questionable. My parents insisted on taking me to Connecticut. It also gave them a chance to visit my aunt and uncle.

My dad parked near the welcome sign. I unloaded my suitcase, poked fun at my brothers and kissed my parents good-bye, but asked them to wait a minute, while I made sure there was, in fact, a job for me here.

Although eager to make money, I was already not thrilled to be here. In some ways, returning from a date on the New York City subway system at midnight frightened me less than when I realized I was being left alone in the Connecticut wilderness to spend ten days as some stranger's employee. To be hired at 16 in New York City required applying for "working papers" and a physical exam. Work hours were limited by law. Connecticut was apparently not concerned about child labor.

Reality began to hit me. This was creepy. I did not know where I was going to sleep and I didn't even have my car. What if I needed to get out of here? When my uncle made the arrangements for my employment here, all was transacted by telephone. There was no formal confirmation, except for what my uncle was told. Nothing on paper. Mistakes could happen and this was no place to be stranded. My parents offered me some comfort by reminding me that my aunt and uncle lived close by if I needed anything. I insisted my parents wait, while I confirmed my employment.

I followed the sign along a path to the office entrance of what was indeed the main building, carrying my suitcase with me. I passed through two sets of glass-paned doors into what I assumed to be the main lobby. It was small and had bright red carpet, looking just like what I imagined an old hotel lobby should look like, with an accompanying musty smell. There were half a dozen upholstered chairs along three walls and a counter on the fourth wall with a small open room and switchboard behind it. To the left of the counter were more glass-paned doors leading into a long hallway that went back to guest rooms on the first floor. I walked up to the counter and politely introduced myself to the only person there. "Hi, I'm Ken Laytin. I'm here to be a busboy." I received a lukewarm look from the small, fair-skinned, older woman with thinning hair that was stiff, puffy and rather blue. You could see through her hair to her scalp. She clearly had returned only minutes before from a hair salon. She told me to sit down and wait and then went back to her work in the room behind the counter. I said I'd be right back. Leaving my suitcase behind, I went out to tell my parents they could go and to remind them to pick me up a week from Sunday after lunch. Everyone was waving as my family drove off.

New Yorkers are famously geocentric. That means we are convinced that New York is the center of the universe and that if you go too far from New York City, you will fall off the edge of the Earth. This place was over 100 miles from New York. Very dangerous. My parents were on their way. Here I was, alone in Connecticut.

Leaving my suitcase unattended for a moment, even in Connecticut, was a big step for me, having grown up in

New York. So when I returned to the lobby, I was relieved to find it still there. I attempted to strike up conversation with the woman behind the counter. Being from the Bronx, that is, being outgoing and fundamentally friendly, added to the fact that I was a bit nervous, made chatting with her seem like the thing to do. Plus, the sooner I learned what was in store for me, the sooner I could begin to relax. But I found myself the only one talking. At no time did I receive a "Welcome to the Teitelman's Inn" or "Where are you from?" or "How was your trip up?" No nothing. So I just sat there growing ever more anxious about what I had gotten myself into. I did get an "Oh" and she perked up slightly when I said I was Phil Franklin's nephew. "Someone should be coming along shortly to take you to the dining room," she said. "Leave your suitcase here, behind the counter. You can pick it up later." My instinct was to ask for a claim check, but I kept it under control.

After what seemed like a very long ten minutes, during which the blue-haired woman never spoke to me again and no one passed through the lobby, a younger man came hurrying through the doors, a bit out of breath. He looked at me and then introduced himself as Henry Baker. He knew instinctively that I was a busboy. This man was more polite and more outgoing than the older woman. He shook my hand and told me to call him Hank. He asked my name and where I came from. He was curious how I happened to be coming all the way from New York City to work here. I told him I was Phil Franklin's nephew. I expected that would impress him. He had never heard of Phil Franklin. Hank explained that he was the local high school science teacher and that he often helped out at the hotel. He almost seemed to be apologizing. Hank was in his mid-thirties, a nice looking man, except that he carried an enormous belly. His right hand seemed to shake. His eyes and his expression were friendly, as were his questions, and so my very first impression of him was positive. I liked science and he was a science teacher. I was now beginning to relax a bit.

We left the Main House and he escorted me from the front office down the walk toward the dining room, one of the white, wooden buildings with the green Hamster Habitat tubes protruding from both sides. The snow was crunchy as we walked along. I asked him who the woman was at the front desk. He said that was Mrs. Teitelman, or Mrs. T. as most people called her. Mr. and Mrs. Teitelman owned the hotel. Hank did not say much else along the way, but even so I was already feeling a bit better about this busboy job I was about to undertake. Then Hank asked me a strange question. He asked if I had brought along a jock strap. My Uncle Phil had told me that the hotel had an enclosed pool, but he warned me that busboys worked long, hard hours. I had not planned to do any swimming. At 16, I was not exactly comfortable with the concept of a jock strap, nor did I want to discuss my underwear with a perfect stranger even if he was a science teacher. Very disturbed by Hank's question, I said "no, why?" "Because we're gonna break your balls" he said.

When we got to the dining room, Hank dropped me off without coming in. He told me to go through the dining room to the far end and into the kitchen and ask the chef for lunch. "Other boys should be arriving soon," he said. I opened one of the big, glass-paned double doors, hesitating as I entered. The room was dimly lit and stuffed with never ending rows of mostly bare, round wooden tables surrounded by wooden chairs with green vinyl seats. With all of the drapes pulled, the room was hard to navigate. There was light toward the other end. I moved across the room with caution. Seeing some people sitting and eating at a table in the one partially lit corner of the room, I approached them and said "Hello." They seemed to ignore me. Perhaps they did not hear me. I repeated "Hello." No one returned my "Hello" but someone at the table glanced at me very briefly, then spoke up and told me go into the kitchen and ask the chef for lunch. He pointed to the kitchen.

I entered the kitchen through a big, swinging wooden door labeled "In." The upper part of the door had a tiny window. The lower part was heavily upholstered in green, tufted vinyl. I was nervous as I entered. I had never seen such a huge kitchen before. The ceilings must have been 20 feet high. Looking across the kitchen, I could see a long stainless steel counter that separated you from a wall of big gas stoves. It was winter, but the kitchen was hot. Three Chinese men were cooking at the stoves behind the counter, each dressed in chef's costumes. They wore bandanas around their necks and were sweating a lot. There were currents of steam rising everywhere, accompanied by the banging and clanging noises of pots and pans being moved around. What voices could be heard were not speaking English. Approaching the counter, I tried making steady eye contact to get someone's attention. When that failed, I tried a traditional, loud, New York "Excuse me." One of the Chinese men turned and said something I did not understand. My response was to tell him I was told to ask for lunch. "For you?" he said. "Yes," I responded. Evidently who it was for made a difference. Offering me no choices, he gave me a plate of something that appeared to be meatloaf.

I don't eat meatloaf. Already I had my first serious problem at the hotel. A friend of my mother's once served me meatloaf with a hardboiled egg looking out at me from the center of my slice. I gagged and refused to eat it. That went over well with my parents. It was also the end of meatloaf for the rest of my life. (In fact, that experience contributed toward my becoming a vegetarian a few decades later). Right now I was hungry and the potatoes and vegetables on the plate looked okay, at least the ones that had not in any way touched the meatloaf. This one had no egg peeking out, but with meatloaf crossed off my list of food fit for human consumption, anything that came into contact with it I classified as contaminated. Nor did I like the smell. I wanted to dump the meatloaf but I had no place to put it where they would not see me do it. So I took my food, thanked him and then looked around the kitchen. Just the potato and veggies were not going to be enough to eat. I looked for bread, having grown up eating lots of bread with every meal. There was a table at the entrance to the kitchen that must have been the official bread table. It was littered with bread, not all of it bagged. I took a few pieces of rye bread from one of the unopened bags. Spotting a yellow, plastic pitcher of iced tea that felt cold, I poured some into what I hoped was a clean glass. Little did I know at the time that obtaining things I was willing to eat at this hotel was going to be a never-ending challenge. And then a strange thought. If these Chinese men were the chefs, how was this a kosher hotel? DeWitt Clinton High School in the Bronx, the school I had attended, had a population of over 6,000 students, a true New York City melting pot. I knew kids from all over the Earth and a few from elsewhere. But I'd never met a Chinese Jew, let alone a Chinese Jew who kept kosher.

Preparing to consume my vegetables, bread and iced tea, I exited the kitchen through the other big green swinging door, the "Out" door, and proceeded toward the table where the people were sitting, the same people who had ignored me a few minutes earlier. There were two empty seats at that table. The group included several fellows a bit older than me who were eating. One appeared by his clothing to be a waiter, another was about Hank Baker's age. He had a loud, crude laugh and was seriously balding. His hair was parted just above his left ear so no one would know. As I approached, it was clear that I was the only one having meatloaf. They had roast beef. Never shy, I asked to join them. The rest of this enormous dining room was dark and empty and it felt less uncomfortable asking to join them, then sitting alone at a bare table. The loud man with the comb-over told me to sit elsewhere, that this was the "Family Table." So I picked a dimly lit table about three rows over that had a used tablecloth on it and sat down. No one asked who I was and no one seemed to care. I could have been a homeless person who just wandered in off the road for free meatloaf. Evidently, either Mrs. Teitelman had called them to warn of my arrival or somehow they could tell either by the lost expression on my face or my naïve attempt to sit at the Family Table that I was a new busboy. Or perhaps the meatloaf gave me away.

Sitting alone, picking through the potatoes and vegetables trying to avoid the meatloaf and any vegetables that might have inadvertently touched it or sat in the juice it exuded, I wondered what happens next. Within only minutes I got my answer. Other meatloaf recipients began to arrive. They must have come in through a back entrance to the kitchen, since they appeared meatloaf in hand. Several of them sat down at my table. Most of those that tried to say hello to the people at the Family Table got little response. One or two got a nod. Some seemed to know not to bother. Others sat at tables neighboring mine. Lots of introductions were exchanged and we all began to talk.

While the arrival of others my age reduced my anxiety level a little, I was having a hard time with the now pervasive aroma of meatloaf. It's hard to eat potatoes, talk and hold your breath at the same time. As I assumed, most of the boys that were wandering in were waiters or busboys. A couple of them were bellhops. Everyone seemed to be between 16 and 20.

Not everyone was new to the hotel. Some of the boys had worked there before and, of course, the locals knew each other. A few came from other parts of Connecticut; one was from Maine. But most lived within the local town. Hank had been instrumental in gathering some of them from Kirby High School to help staff the hotel for the holiday week. That was part of his job. He'd actually gotten them released early from school that day and sent them to the hotel. In Kirby, farm boys became busboys for the holiday week. This was evidently a common occurrence whenever the Teitelman's Inn was open for a holiday. However, since not all Jewish holidays corresponded to school vacation days in Connecticut, it seems the farm boys not only left school early, but that they often missed classes when Hank assigned them to work at the hotel. That might be why Hank had some success recruiting. Or perhaps Teitelman's Inn had an arrangement with the Connecticut Board of Education when busboys were needed.

Having introduced myself to the other busboys, I discretely pointed to the man who had already begun to growl at me when I had tried to sit at his table. I asked who he was. Someone told me that he was Mr. and Mrs. Teitelman's son, Martin, the boss of the kitchen and dining room. Known generally as Martin, though sometimes as "MT", he was our boss. He ran the dining room and kitchen, overseeing the food purchases, the kitchen staff and all of us. His mother, Mrs. T., the lady with the puffy, stiff, blue hair, ran the office and reservations. Mr. Morris Teitelman, her husband, known as Morris T. or Mr. T., ran the grounds keeping, maintenance and the hotel in general. Mr. and Mrs. T. lived in the colonial home I had spotted up on the hill. Martin and his second wife lived in a home down the road. They clearly had more to tell me about Martin, but this was not the time or place.

Before long Martin got up from his table and began to

chat with some of the fellows in the room; he obviously knew some of them. My table received no introduction from Martin, however, and still no welcome to the Teitelman's Inn. He wasn't even interested in our names. He merely took visual inventory of his staff, like a bitch counting its puppies, but without the love or the bond. Martin told us to hurry up and finish eating, take our empty plates and glasses to the rear of the kitchen to be washed, strip any linen from our tables, take it to the linen room and then return to our seats immediately. Martin returned to the Family Table. As I watched Martin walk around the dining room, there was something about him I already did not like. He was about 5' 9", with a slightly pudgy face, weak shoulders and a rather non-athletic appearance. "Stuck up" seemed like an appropriate description, not just from his attitude, but also from the way he walked. It all went well with the comb-over.

Once we were all back in our seats, a fellow of some apparent rank began to talk to us, directing much of his eye contact toward those of us he did not recognize. He said he was the captain of the dining room, whatever that meant. He walked around us with his clipboard identifying how many of us the hotel expected had actually shown up as well as who was a waiter and who was a busboy, with or without experience. He asked the names of the boys he did not recognize. When he asked my name, he inquired if I had any experience as a waiter or busboy in a hotel or a restaurant. I said no. Then he began assigning busboys to waiters. He told me that I would be working for Sal, a fellow who was sitting at another table. More specifically, while chuckling, he told me that I was "Sal's slave." Sal was the waiter and I was assigned to him.

Sal too appeared to hold some rank at the hotel in that he immediately made it very clear to the captain and everyone else that he was not happy about getting me, an inexperienced busboy. His objection to me was loud and his arms were waiving when they weren't pointing at me. The captain told him there were not enough experienced busboys to go around, but assured him that if someone better showed up he would get to trade me. That certainly made me feel valued.

I learned from the other boys that Sal's clout, or at least his right to complain publicly, derived partly from his experience, but mainly from the fact that his father was the current #1 chef, the Chinese man who gave me the meatloaf. It still made no sense that Chinese men were the chefs at a kosher hotel. I'd seen Jewish people in Chinese restaurants, but never the other way around. Sal did not exactly look Chinese, either. His eyes were narrow, but his skin was medium brown and his hair dark but wavy. When I quietly asked one of the other busboys about Sal, he told me that although the Chinese chef was indeed Sal's father, Sal's mother was Puerto

Rican. Sal's full name was Salvador Wang.

Suddenly, Martin stood up, abruptly interrupted his captain, demanded our attention and spoke to the group. His speech was mostly about rules related to our appearance, our handling of reusable food, about the strict prohibition against waiters and busboys eating "guest" food and about the prohibition of females in our rooms. It was a long list of what we were not allowed to do. Everything he said sounded like a threat. Now I was certain that Martin was a jerk. He was loud, arrogant and revealed no interest in us as humans. He seemed to be anticipating the worst behavior from us, perhaps based upon experience with his waiters and busboys, but I was still annoyed at having been humiliated when I tried earlier to take a seat at his table.

After this lecture by Martin on the long list of hotel rules, the captain resumed the assignments. Busboys then went off with the waiter they were assigned to. Sal and I sat down in the area that we would be serving from. He told me more about what was expected of me, trying to encapsulate his wealth of waiter and busboy knowledge into a 30-minute Cliff's Notes version. He showed me our tables and then told me to meet him back here in one hour in my uniform for more detailed training. He would get me a busboy jacket. First, Hank the science teacher would show those of us who were sleeping at the hotel to our rooms. I was hoping my suitcase was still where I left it.

The hotel had an official "Staff House" conveniently located between the rear of the kitchen and the abandoned chicken coops. During this holiday week in December, 1965 the heat in Staff House was turned off. It was too costly to the Teitelmans to leave it on. Hank told us how lucky we were, implying something about the Staff House. Since most of the boys working the holiday week lived close enough to go home each night, the few of us who needed rooms were going to be permitted to stay in the Main House for the week.

The Main House was the old three-story wooden building where Hank had found me earlier after I met Mrs. T., the woman with blue hair. It was the hotel's original building. It housed the main office, the bookkeeper's office, the switchboard and had guest quarters on all three floors. Clearly a firetrap, it offered the least expensive guestrooms. I was getting to stay in a guestroom. Downstairs, through the doors beyond the front desk, were some of the more pleasant guestrooms. Upstairs were the hotel guests who wanted the cheapest rooms. I learned soon after that these were the same guests who depended heavily on prunes and prune juice. Often they had difficulty making it up the stairs to their rooms, so my room would be on the very top floor.

While a bit concerned about ever getting out alive in the event of a fire, I found the accommodations acceptable under the circumstances. I did make note of where the fire escape was. At least I had a single room. The shared bathroom was down the hall, but my room had its own sink. Other busboys had already told me how awful the Staff House was. "Consider yourself very lucky," they said. Perhaps, I thought, this was a vestige of my uncle's influence. But I learned later it was only because the Staff House had no insulation and the hotel was not full. I unpacked my stuff in this tiny private room, tried to relax and enjoy my partially obstructed view of Lake Gilmer, thought about my parents and brothers on their way back to New York City and wondered how much money I was about to make in my ten days as Sal's non-preferred busboy. I hoped that some of my experiences growing up would be useful in helping me master the soon-to-be-acquired skills of a busboy.

2
HOW TO BE A BUSBOY

I was born in the Bronx, where I spent my childhood and most of my teenage years. We lived on the third floor of a well-maintained, six-story, rent-controlled apartment building, set among similar buildings and some two-story brick, private homes. At street level, the building was populated with stores, including a drug store, a grocer, a shoemaker, a butcher and a television repair shop. I had my own bedroom with a corner window. It gave me a lovely view of West Burnside Avenue, including the luncheonette, beauty salon, hardware store, Chinese laundry, bakery and kosher delicatessen, as well as the cars, city buses and partially paved-over cobblestone streets and trolley car tracks. My elementary school, Public School 26, was only three blocks away and could be seen from my bedroom window. My junior high school, Macombs Junior High School 82, was only five blocks away. I took a city bus and/or a subway to Dewitt Clinton High School. I played stick ball and dodge ball in the streets, rode my green Royce Union three-speed bike among the cars and hung out on street corners with dozens of kids my age. This past fall, at age 16, I began attending New York University, whose "uptown" campus was a green oasis in the middle of a concrete and brick neighborhood. The NYU campus was only three blocks away, within easy walking distance of our apartment.

I did have some experience in non-urban environments, since for many of my summers growing up, my parents, my younger fraternal twin brothers and I had vacationed in New York's Catskill Mountains, either staying at kosher hotels or in what were called bungalow colonies. Bungalow colonies were clusters of perhaps 15 to 30 rental cottages that belonged to one owner and offered communal tennis courts, a swimming pool, a Social Hall, a food concession, a phone booth and so forth. The part of the Catskill mountain area of New York State we vacationed in is called the "Borscht Belt." It was nicknamed after a soup consumed by people of Russian and Eastern European descent who brought it to America. While there are many recipe variations of borscht that include potato, celery, carrots, onion and seasonings, its main ingredient is beets. It is served cold, often in a glass, and has sour cream mixed in just before being served, creating a red and white suspension straight out of chemistry class. Many of the Catskill area hotels provided menus which catered to Jews of European ancestry, and had well-known Jewish comedians and entertainers appearing, such as Jack Benny, Sid Caesar, Buddy Hackett, Red Buttons, Mel Brooks and Jackie Mason. Our seasonal foray each summer to the Catskills was our escape from the hot New York City streets. It almost seemed that these places existed just to get kids out of the city for part or all of the summer.

Our family, as was typical of many middle-class families seeking to escape the New York City summer, had mom and the kids in the Catskills, with dad remaining in the city. He drove the 100 miles up on Friday nights after work and headed back to New York City early on Monday mornings. He only spent a full week with us if he could take a vacation. During my early teens, I was a guest along with my parents in several of these large, kosher hotels in the Catskills. That made me slightly familiar with how a hotel dining room operated, at least enough to take on the role of busboy at such a place, or so I thought. My brothers and I often looked up to the college-age waiters and busboys at the places we stayed, like the Aladdin Hotel in Woodbourne and the Delano Hotel in Monticello, so taking such a job seemed really cool to me.

Teitelman's Inn, however, was not in the Catskills. It was in the dead center of nowhere in Connecticut. But like hotels in New York's Catskill Mountains, it was mainly a summer resort, though it opened briefly for major American and Jewish holidays during the rest of the year. They must have gotten the idea to do that from the 1942 movie "Holiday Inn," starring Bing Crosby, Fred Astaire and Marjorie Reynolds.

Being anxious about my new job, I returned a bit early to the dining room. Having changed clothes, I was wearing the silly outfit my uncle told me to bring along. Sal was already there. He found a red busboy's jacket for me. It was of the coolie type, buttoning up the neck at the side. More Chinese influence, I figured. I had been advised by my uncle to come to the hotel with black tuxedo pants, white shirts, black shoes, black socks, a black bow tie and a cummerbund. I borrowed my father's cummerbund. My parents had to buy me the rest of the costume. How many 16-year-olds own tuxedo pants and a bow tie? So here I am all dressed up. The red jacket completed my outfit. However, with the buttons going all of the way up the front and then up the side of the collar, it hid the white shirt, bow tie and cummerbund so well they were not necessary. I could have worn just black tuxedo pants and a tee shirt. Not so for the waiters, whose gold jackets were cut in the front like tuxedo "tails" Fred Astaire wore in the movies, with big lapels, showing off the bow tie and cummerbund and making them look classy. No tails in the back, however. Their gold tuxedo jackets were fastened with gold (polished brass) buttons. The costumes alone made the supervisor-supervisee relationship clear. Only the addition of a college fraternity pledge beanie with a propeller on top could have made me look more stupid.

Sal said that we had only two hours until the hotel guests would arrive for their first dinner of this ten-day Christmas through New Year's holiday. We would have to be ready to serve our first meal together. We would be working out of a 2' by 3' by 5' tall wooden serving station he called a server. It had an open shelf inside for a bus box used to collect dirty dishes, a shallow shelf above that, two drawers below for silverware, one for meat and one for dairy, a broad flat top for the waiter to put his tray on, and a small open section at the bottom for spare napkins. The maître d' and captain would assign people to our tables and we would be serving those same people three meals each day for their entire ten-day stay. We might also be assigned people who came just for one evening. They were referred to as "D.O.s." No, they were not Doctors of Osteopathy; they were people who came for "Dinner Only," plus the evening entertainment. I figured this couldn't be too hard. Sal had to bring them their food and I would do the cleanup. If old men waiters and bleached blondes with too much makeup could practically throw the food at people in kosher deli's in New York City and still get tips, I, a college student at NYU, could certainly succeed in a kosher hotel in Connecticut. But Sal disagreed. "I had a lot to learn" he said, as he tried to impart more of his years of experience to me in an ultra-condensed form.

Sal began by explaining where busboys really fit in, as if I had not already deduced that by the rather limited welcome upon my arrival, the meat loaf and my costume. If one were to rank order the hotel staff from most important to least important, he explained, number one would be the first chef (in this case his father), then the salad/pantry man, then the second chef, breakfast chef, chefs' helpers, pantry help, dishwashers, pot washers, then waiters, then bellhops and finally busboys. I was an inexperienced busboy.

It was interesting to be lower on the totem than the pot washers. They were generally ex-cons, genuine bums, homeless men, current or former mental patients or any combination of the above. Sal said that Martin would drive to New York's Bowery with a station wagon and literally hire men off the sidewalks. He promised them three meals a day, somewhere to sleep and Sal assumed Martin promised them booze. He didn't know if Martin offered them money. As a busboy, Sal explained, I was less important. I was replaceable, but pot washers were hard to come by in Connecticut. Sal then detailed my job.

I was to set all dishes before the meal. He taught me what the different size dishes were called – mains, flats, soups, number ones, and miniature soup bowls he called "monkey dishes." He showed me how to place them and which ones were there for appearance only and would be removed as the meal began. Just before the guests arrived, I was to bring out baskets of bread, butter dishes, pickle dishes, milkers, creamers and water pitchers. During the meal, my job was to remove all finished dishes and refill baskets of bread, butter dishes, pickle dishes, milkers, creamers and water pitchers, as needed. I would also serve beverages. Both during and after the meal, I'd pack all used dishes into bus boxes and take them to be washed. Multiple trips would be required. After the meal, I would sweep and vacuum, clean ashtrays, clean crumbs off the chairs and empty water pitchers. I would also do an unending variety of unpaid jobs around the dining room between meals called "side jobs." These might include loading dishes into the warmers for the chefs, removing linen from the big bags that were delivered and onto the shelves in the linen room and even helping the captain's busboy, since the captain did not do his own work but rather delegated all but serving his guests to his and other busboys. Side jobs would be assigned to me by the captain.

When we had a moment, I asked Sal why the little bowl was called a "monkey dish." He explained that there were several theories of where the name came from. It might have been a bowl the size a monkey would use. It might have been a bowl that was originally made from a monkey's skull, or it was the size of the cup a monkey held to collect tips for an organ grinder in the 1800's. But the most likely explanation was that kings and queens once had small portions of their food fed to monkeys to be sure it wasn't poisoned. I was impressed with Sal's knowledge.

Sal continued, explaining to me that when a guest was

done eating, his plate was always to be removed from the right. I was never to reach across someone to clear a dish. Guests were never to be rushed, but they did not like having dirty dishes sitting in front of them either. I had to get the timing right. Don't scoop it the moment they are done, but don't leave it there too long either. I was never to pile up dirty dishes on the table in front of a guest. No one liked to have someone else's leftovers placed in front of them. Any stacking of dirty dishes should be on my arm, behind the guests. All beverages were to be served to the guest's right. Being the waiter, Sal's job was to set linen, silverware and glasses, unless he told me to do it. He would serve all food. I was never to serve food unless Sal directed me to do so. A busboy serving food, he said, could "cut" the waiter's tips. I had no idea what that meant.

Next, Sal decided to take me into the kitchen to meet his father. Busboys, he said, were sometimes sent to the kitchen by their waiter to make "exchanges" when the waiter brought the guest the wrong food or the guest found fault with the food. In this way, the chefs would scream (in Chinese, of course) at the busboy instead of the waiter. That explained why Sal wanted to identify me to his father. He appeared to have to urge him to be nice to me. Based on his father's body language, I was not convinced that he had agreed. Sal explained that the less time a busboy spent on voyages to and from the distant end of the kitchen with his bus boxes, the more he was available to help his waiter and the better the service the clientele got. My job during the meal was not merely to take the heavy bus boxes full of dirty dishes back to the kitchen, but rather to run back with them and then run back to the dining room with empty ones. Better service also meant making sure that all dishes, glasses and silverware we set out were clean. No crud and no water spots. It meant bringing coffee and tea whenever a guest wanted some and generally minimizing the time people were kept waiting for anything they had requested, all while being neat and courteous. I was to be visually scanning all of our tables constantly to see if someone was trying to get our attention. Again, better service meant better tips. But if they asked me for something that was Sal's responsibility, I was to find him immediately and let him know. I was not to serve it myself, unless he told me to do so. Above all, never spill anything on anyone.

Sal warned me that if I did spill food or worse yet hot coffee on a guest and they complained loudly, Martin would likely come running over. If the guest appeared unhappy enough, Martin would fire me on the spot. But not to worry, Sal said. The "firing" was a charade designed to make the guest feel guilty, since they knew many of us were college kids. Martin would insist on the firing until the guest begged him not to. He'd then call the busboy (or waiter) over to apologize again to the guest. When the kiss kiss, hug hug was over, I'd still have a job, probably, unless it happened often.

The next lesson involved teaching me to arrange the dirty dishes within a bus box so as to take as many dishes as possible on each trip. Main dish plates standing on edge could be arranged around the inside perimeter of the bus box and built up like bricks in a running bond to raise the side walls higher. That made it possible to fill the box higher and higher with dirty dishes, well beyond the top of the box, higher than the box was designed for. Fewer trips to the kitchen meant more availability to help the waiter keep the guests happy. But stacked this way, the boxes could get quite heavy and difficult to raise up out of the serving station and onto your shoulder. Still, it was more efficient, he insisted, than going all the way back to the kitchen with a partially full box. The box was always to be carried on my shoulder, not carried in front of me. More professional looking and less chance of a hernia that way, he explained. Perhaps that was why Hank had inquired about the jock strap. Sometimes the bus box was so heavy that the waiter needed to help hoist it to your shoulder.

Sal also directed me not to talk to the guests much or be too friendly. That was his job. He explained that normally guests tip the waiter and busboy separately in a 3-2 ratio, and that if a busboy was too friendly or served a noticeable amount of the food, he could alter the proportion, increasing his own tip and reducing the waiter's. That was what he meant earlier by "cutting" your waiter. We, of course, did not want that to happen. So the two things in this entire place I actually knew how to do, talk and be friendly, I was told not to do.

The two hours of our setup work and training passed quickly. Tablecloths were on the tables. Linen napkins were set out. I carried all the dishes from the kitchen and positioned them on the tables as Sal had shown me. There were main dishes with both flat plates and soup bowls set inside them. They weren't going to be used. They were only there to make the table look nice when the people sat down. I'd take them back to the kitchen once Sal began serving. Sal set out the glasses and double silverware. Two forks sitting on a folded linen napkin to the left of the main dish plate, with the inside fork positioned higher than the outside one. To the right, a knife, a soup spoon, another knife and then two teaspoons. One teaspoon higher than the other. Fancy equaled better tips. In order to make certain nothing we set out had any crud or water spots, I was to carry a white linen napkin folded neatly hanging out of my back pocket. I could use it to clean anything not up to standard. This napkin, known as a side towel, gradually became a dirty rag. But you kept cleaning with it. Finally, we were all set. Our tables looked good. Though nervous, I was eager for the meal to start. Sal was sweating like his father back in the kitchen.

3
MY FIRST MEAL

Sal and I worked our first meal together that evening. It was a nightmare. Our guests were crazy. I could see the disaster coming the moment the guests began to arrive. Generally, all of the hotel's 300-350 guests entered the dining room at the same time for each meal. They gathered at the front door of the dining room or in the hamster tunnels waiting for the dining room to open. Then they rushed in. The waiters called it "post time." When the maître d' opened the dining room doors, you would think the 5:00 whistle had just blown at a GM assembly plant. Except in a Japanese Godzilla movie, I had never seen so many people heading so rapidly in one direction. Anyone foolish enough to stand by the door could have been trampled to death. Some guests already knew their table assignments for the week; others crowded around the maître d' to find out.

Martin Teitelman stood in people's way trying to greet them. Most were interested in the food, not in Martin. His loud voice and coarse laugh only added to the confusion. When our guests were finally all seated at their assigned tables, that is, our tables, the look on Sal's face quickly told me that we had more people to serve than Sal was prepared for, despite his experience and connections in the kitchen.

Sal introduced himself and then sort of introduced me. It made no difference to some of our guests. They didn't give a shit who we were. They were hungry. Some of our guests were crabby and began to complain within five minutes of being seated. Some didn't like their table. They would have preferred one along the window or closer to the aisle. Some thought the dining room was too cold. Once Sal started serving, some complained about how long they waited for each successive course.

At a restaurant, people arrive in small groups and at different times and are, therefore, staggered with respect to what course they are on relative to people sitting near them. Not so at the hotel. Three hundred and fifty people expect the same course at about the same time. Except someone is always first when you serve and someone is always last. If you have five tables of eight guests each, the fifth table starts to notice they are last. This is even more problematic when the tables they are near belong to a different waiter who is serving those tables first or second. But then not only were many of our guests cranky about not being served first, many found fault with various items Sal finally served them. For me, the problem was less the cranky guests than the bus boxes. With dishes stacked the way Sal told me to do it, the boxes of dirty dishes were so heavy that I had to squat down and have Sal slide the box out of our serving station and onto my shoulder.

Sal had neglected to tell me that many bus boxes had holes or cracks in them. The cracks allowed the slop of leftover foods that slid off the dishes to the bottom of the box to leak out all over my shoulder and down the back of my clean red jacket, as I attempted to run, overloaded, to the kitchen. I also left a trail of liquid schmutz staining the carpeting behind me along the way.

When I got to the dishwasher area of the kitchen, it was difficult to find room among the other bus boxes to put mine down, even if there was someone willing to help me get it off my shoulder. While struggling with the bus box at the back of the kitchen, I tried to hold my breath in an effort to escape the awful smell coming from the huge dirty pots sitting on the sinks and floor along with the accumulating dirty dishes. No wonder pot washers were hard to come by. They had to be anosmic. But holding your breath was difficult after running with a very heavy box on your shoulder.

 Each trip to the rear of the kitchen had me gone from the dining room a long time. Dozens of people were waiting for coffee, tea and other beverages that I was responsible for serving. Not yet having learned to run with five hot cups of coffee, I could only carry two cups at one time. And even that was awkward. People wanted their dirty dishes cleared immediately. Throughout the meal, Sal was unhappy with me. While his comments came in the form of whispers, they clearly conveyed anger and frustration. Nothing I did was fast enough. It was amazing. The kitchen was slow, I was too slow and the guests were in a big hurry.

By the time the ordeal of our first meal was over, I was exhausted. My red jacket, clean at the beginning of the meal, now had a disgusting mess on the left shoulder and down the back. I had to wear it for most of the week. Replacements would not be available until next weekend.

In addition to not letting me know that bus boxes leaked, Sal had neglected to advise me to cover my shoulder with a linen napkin before we hoisted up the bus box. I wondered if he had forgotten on purpose. If I looked like a slob for the week, I'd be less likely to cut his tips. Nor was his ten second lesson before the meal successful at teaching me how to carry five or six hot cups of coffee at one time and run. That skill required years of practice while wearing a fireproof wet suit.

I did learn quickly, however, to load and carry my bus box so as not to get a hernia, and how to carry it on my left shoulder although I was right handed. This way my right hand was free to push guests or staff out of my way to avoid a fatal collision. Sal taught me how to set tables and most importantly, as far as the hotel was concerned, which items left on the table at the end of a meal were to be returned to the kitchen for reuse at a later meal.

Few people know that Teitelman's Inn invented the concept of recycling. The items we were required to recycle were known as "livestock." A funny term, I thought, but it must have been the local farm influence. Livestock included anything that had been placed on the table family style, such as bread, cheese, butter, milk, cream, pickles and coleslaw, but only if they were still in the original dish they were served in. They were to be returned to the kitchen immediately after a meal even if they had sat out for hours. That someone may have stuck a used spoon or fork into them was never considered. That even in Connecticut there were bacteria, was never considered. These leftovers were either recycled into a future meal for the guests or, once the bacteria count had grown high enough, given to the waiters and busboys to consume the next day.

Since returning livestock to the kitchen was time consuming and seemed unsanitary, and since the waiters and busboys did not want to consume milk re-chilled after it sat out for two or three hours or bread that was hard, Sal advised me to dump all livestock into my bus boxes with the dirty dishes. Doing so, however, a behavior known as "killing livestock" was a sin management would punish by firing the sinner. If I did kill livestock, Sal said, "Be sure to break it or crush it beyond recognition." Food in the bus box had to look at least partially eaten, since Martin would randomly follow us into the kitchen to see if we were killing livestock.

Whole pickles or slices of bread in your bus box could be used as evidence against you. Broken ones could not. Similarly, discarding linen napkins by throwing them in with the dirty dishes was a capital crime, although a lot easier and less time consuming than shaking them out and returning them to the dirty linen room.

While dumping butter, milk, cream and pickles into your bus box had labor saving advantages, doing so carried a risk almost as frightening as being fired. It was the tsunami of kosher liquids that occurred inside the bus box when you tried to balance it on your shoulder and run to the kitchen. The undulating liquids made the bus box very unstable on your shoulder, greatly increasing the risk of a major disaster while virtually guaranteeing a river of pickle juice and milk running over your shoulder and down the back of your jacket. As much as Sal impressed upon me the rules of conduct as they related to the performance of my job as a busboy, it was clear that when we got busy, as far as he was concerned all rules could be abandoned, even at the risk of being fired. But whenever Sal encouraged me to break sacred rules, I could not help but wonder if he was teaching me the way it really was or if he was trying to get me fired so he could get a better busboy. They couldn't fire him, however, because if they did, his father, the Chinese kosher chef might quit.

As the week continued, I learned that during a meal,

busboys were often called upon to perform not only their official duties, but whatever else their waiter needed them to do, particularly if the waiter was "hanging." Hanging occurred when the waiter had too many people to serve, when he was disorganized or incompetent, because the kitchen was very slow that meal, or any combination of the above. It meant that the waiter's guests were furious because he was serving them their meal a course or two behind the other few hundred people eating in the dining room, even though everyone had been seated at once. Sal and I "hung" at our first meal and at almost every meal. I think it was less because Sal was a bad waiter than because he was assigned too many tables, had some very complaining guests and had a bad busboy. By the time our guests got their soup, it seemed like most everyone else was eating dessert.

To keep guests happy, Sal always tried to be one of the first waiters on line in the kitchen. So did every other waiter. He took orders from the guests as fast as he could and then ran to the kitchen. So did every other waiter. But if our guests arrived even a minute late or were slow getting to their tables when the dining room doors opened and the starting bell rang, Sal would be late getting into the kitchen for appetizers. Then he would be late getting in for soup and then late getting in for main dishes. If he ended up near the end of main dish line, he risked the kitchen running out of an item.

That required going back to our tables, having to apologize and make up some bullshit story like "The lamb chop truck broke down" and then taking orders all over again. Guests were even less happy than before once this happened because they were now waiting even longer and for their *second* choice. When six of the eight guests at a table arrived on time, but the last couple was late, it produced even more chaos. Not only was Sal no longer on the same course with all of our tables, but now not even within a table. He would have me serving the couple of late comers. But when he sent me, other guests were kept waiting for coffee or to have their dirty dishes cleared.

Normally, the waiter needs to have all of his tables on the same course at once. He makes one or two runs to the kitchen for appetizers, one or two runs for soups, and then takes main dish orders from one table at a time and races to the kitchen. He waits on a line of waiters until his turn. He tells the chef his eight (or 10 or 12 if a big table) orders and waits as the chef plates each one for him. He stacks them on his tray, lifts it to his shoulder and races out of the kitchen to serve the food. If an entire table arrives late or, worse yet, if a few individuals at any one table arrive late, they are out of sequence with the rest of the tables and automatically initiate our hanging at that meal.

When we were hanging, all hotel rules, sanitary practices

and religious traditions of separating meat and dairy dishes and silverware were abandoned. You could not serve your guests fast enough to keep them quiet. The guests were like babies; the best way to keep them quiet was to feed them.

I never really understood why people gave us so much grief when we were hanging and they had to wait. It wasn't like they were going anywhere between meals. There was nowhere to go and nothing to do in cold December in the middle of Connecticut. Even the cows were indoors. After each meal, the hotel guests just walked around for a while like little hamsters in the green plastic tunnels. Then they played cards in the Social Hall or took naps and came back through the green tunnels for the next meal. In any event, if they did get mad at you, Sal explained that your tips would suffer. That was why he wanted a super busboy, not me. He needed a busboy who was not only quick, organized and would not attempt to kibitz with the guests, but one who had that indefinable charisma that helped him return alive from the kitchen when the waiter sent him back with an exchange. My only skill initially was the kibitzing, a skill that did not work with the Chinese chefs and as I was regularly reminded, one I was prohibited from displaying with the guests.

I do not want to give the impression that all Chinese chefs belong in state facilities for the criminally insane, but all of the chefs at this place did. Although Sal's father cooperated silently when I requested an exchange, he often looked at me with a stare that gave me a chill. This chef knew the exchange was for his son, but unfortunately nobody told the #2 and #3 chefs. The first time I made an exchange for Sal which required me to ask #2 Chinese chef to swap a medium-well steak for a medium-rare, I put my entire future in jeopardy. The chef took my plate and set up a new one. He then put it down on the long stainless steel counter that separated me from him. Without realizing that he had not yet sprinkled parsley on the potatoes, I tried to pick up the new plate. He immediately made a sincere effort to chop off my right hand with a giant knife, while simultaneously teaching the entire kitchen staff new Chinese curse words. His knife actually hit the counter hard, where my hand had just been.

Sal had already admonished me never to talk back to the chefs when they were screaming at me. Busboys and waiters who defended themselves verbally were now former busboys and waiters. Sal explained that the kitchen was hot and the chefs temperamental. They would easily become so mad at a waiter or busboy that they would refuse to provide him with food for the guests he was serving, or refuse to allow him in the kitchen again altogether. Martin T. saw little use for a waiter who could not obtain food from the kitchen or a busboy who was not allowed in the kitchen. Although I did not understand Chinese, it was easy to tell when the chefs were discussing a waiter's mother.

Normally only dirty dishes went into the bus box. Glasses were returned separately, standing upright on trays, so as not to be broken. Trays of course were carried on your shoulder, just like bus boxes. Again, no sissy carrying of trays in front of you and no hernias. You had to balance the tray full of used glasses at shoulder level with one hand. The other hand opened the kitchen door and/or blocked guests and other waiters or busboys who were about to collide with you.

Sal taught me to pick good trays from the kitchen since some of them would buckle in the middle and pop up and down under the weight of glasses, setting the stage for a disaster. Dirty linen was shaken out at the end of the meal, put into giant laundry bags in the linen room, and sent to the laundry. I was warned never to clean an ash tray after a meal by dumping it into the table cloth and using the cloth to wipe it clean, as it could smolder and later start a fire in the linen room, potentially burning down the hotel. But I saw all of the busboys doing it anyway. Silverware was to be kept separate and the waiter normally stood by in the kitchen, guarding his own, as it was washed in a special machine. Livestock was to be returned as soon as possible. Being a kosher hotel, there were distinct meat and dairy dishes and silverware, which were required to be kept separate.

The hotel was busy my first week there and short a few waiters and busboys. Some of the busboys and waiters who worked during the summer lived out of state and chose not to travel to Connecticut for the Christmas through New Year's week. Hank could only get so many recruits from his high school science classes unless he offered them extra credit. They knew how hard the work was and many preferred to get up at 4:30 a.m. to milk cows over being a busboy.

In a typical summer week, Sal said he would normally handle 24 people at three tables of eight, or 32 seated at four tables of eight if the hotel was very busy. But during holiday periods such as tonight, he had 48 guests spread across six tables. Mrs. T. had taken reservations for a lot of osteopaths that night. Sal said that Mrs. T. never said no to more paying guests for dinner only. Same situation the next night with D.O.s. Breakfasts and lunches were a bit more manageable, with only five tables. But at most meals, my bus boxes became delicate mixtures of dishes, leftover food, glasses, linen napkins and some silverware, all sloshing around in killed livestock. I got away with it all that week. So did every other busboy. It was a week of disorganized chaos. The new busboys just there for the week, like me, had no idea what they were doing. The experienced ones knew exactly what they were supposed to do but did not care. Hank Baker was right about the ball busting, but I made a lot of money, about $125 for the holiday week; enough money to cover the cost of my bow tie and tuxedo pants and motivate me to return for the upcoming full summer season as a very slightly experienced busboy.

4
NOW I AM A BUSBOY

That holiday week in December, 1965, I made what was a lot of money for a 16 year old. Since my NYU tuition and my textbooks were very expensive, I wanted to help my parents pay for some of it. They never demanded I earn money toward tuition, they simply knew I would try to do so. I was always willing to work. Tuition money was not my only objective, however. There was stereo equipment I wanted and there was my $15 1955 Buick Convertible. While now reasonably roadworthy, keeping it that way was an expensive hobby. I decided to return to the Teitelman's Inn for the full summer season. After all, I was now somewhat "experienced." One twist in the driver's license issue in New York was that while normally you could not be fully licensed until 18, at 16 you could drive in less populated parts of New York State. New York City was off limits. But completion of a special driver education course in high school would let me get the full license at 17. I had taken and passed the course, so as the summer of my 17th year approached, I was legal and had a car to go to Connecticut.

The previous December when the Staff House had no heat, I had been permitted to live in the Main House among the guests, as did the few other waiters and busboys who were not local and could not go home each night. In mid June, 1966, when I returned for my first full summer season at the hotel, the accommodations were not quite as luxurious. I was to live in the Staff House, an old barracks-like building on a hill behind the hotel, between the butcher shop and the abandoned chicken coops. The senior waiters, the guys who made serious money, usually joined together in groups of four or five and rented places off grounds. Their Staff House days were behind them. For the rest of us, the Staff House was the only place we could afford.

You entered the Staff House at one end. It was a long, narrow, single-story wooden building with ten "bedrooms" down one side of the hall. As you entered, if you turned right, you looked into the only three showers. If you looked left, you looked into the bathroom with four sinks and four toilets. Further down the hall were the so-called bedrooms. Each was only about 7' X 8' but designed to sleep four with two sets of bunk beds. The bunks were made of 2' X 6's and plywood. Rooms were too small for four guys to dress at the same time each morning without a lot of unwanted ass-to-ass contact. The rooms were too small for closets, dressers or mirrors. The only location for my possessions was the open plywood extension of my top bunk. The mattresses were so disgusting that on my first afternoon there in June, a group of us drove to town to get plastic mattress bags and cans of Lysol at the hardware store. We took our mattresses outside and beat them with big sticks before we saturated them with disinfectant. Then we bagged them before we slept on them.

The competition each morning for the showers, sinks and toilets was fierce. Busboys and waiters had to be clean. We actually underwent fingernail inspections in the dining room on Saturday nights, or whenever the captain or Martin T. needed to feel powerful. While *we* and our outfits were supposed to be clean, the Staff House was filthy. Dirty linen and leftover food was everywhere. It was not uncommon to awaken and see a mouse walking along one of the 2' X 6's that were the frame of my bunk bed.

No women were allowed in the Staff House. Not that any of us were strongly inclined to ever bring a girl there anyway; it was too dirty and we had no privacy. The no women rule did not to apply, however, to an assistant in the pantry named Willie, who occupied one of the rooms at the far end of the hall. Willie was a short, stocky guy, perhaps age 45. He too appeared at least somewhat Asian, with straight, shiny jet black hair. This was not Willie's first season at the hotel. The waiters and busboys who had worked there previously had a history with Willie. It was clear enough that he did not like us and that for many of the boys the feeling was mutual. Some of it was jealousy by the busboys that Willie had a single room. He also had a woman with him. Well, sort of a woman. She was about 40, terribly skinny, ugly, and bow-legged. Her hair was bizarre, wiry, and dyed black. She was weird enough in her affect, her gait and her behavior to make me think now she was probably schizophrenic. It surprised me that she was allowed out during daylight. As strange as she was, however, she would manage to time her wandering down the hall in and out of the Staff House to just when everyone was trying to shower and dress. So before long some of the boys began to entertain her with nudity, noises and obscene gestures. One of the waiters was particularly fond of passing her in the hall while he walked naked, carrying a towel on his erection. One of the other waiters would taunt Willie from afar with "Willie, I love your woman's bo...dy.... heavy duty" when he walked by. This made Willie crazy, and only made life tougher for the rest of us as we tried to conduct business at the kitchen pantry with Willie.

Besides there being no closets or dressers in the Staff House for us to store our stuff, neither the building nor the rooms were ever locked. In addition to Willie and his woman, we shared the building with the less fortunate of the kitchen staff, the pot washers Martin had picked up in the Bowery. They, too, were four to a room. Theft was a regular occurrence in the Staff House. It quickly forced me to store most of my clothing and personal items locked in my 1955 Buick. It was not uncommon to see me getting dressed at 6:30 a.m. in the parking lot behind the kitchen, by the open trunk of my car.

While property theft was a problem in the Staff House, by the end of June I discovered it was an even bigger problem in the dining room, particularly on Saturday nights when the dining room was overbooked with D.O.s. It was not the guests' property or even the staff's property that was being stolen and certainly not the guests doing the stealing. To paraphrase Abe Lincoln, it was hotel property being stolen from the waiters, by the waiters and for the waiters. Actually, theft is the wrong term. It was really socialism, a sort of redistribution of wealth. It was the stuff waiters and busboys needed to serve a meal and they were taking it from one another.

Resources in the dining room could be scarce because the Teitelmans were cheap. The hotel had a sleeping capacity of about 350 and only a slightly greater comfortable seating capacity in the dining room, perhaps 400. Therefore, there were full complements of dishes and silverware for a little over 400 guests when all the settings were done correctly, with fancy dish plates and double forks, knives and spoons. The extra dishes and silverware were intended to cover the D.O.s. Extra tables, both serviceable and broken, were stored below the dining room in the basement. That was the best-case scenario. In reality, at any point in time, missing silverware, broken glasses, broken dishes or wobbly tables would reduce the actual number available. But little old Mrs. Teitelman and her blue hair did not believe in ever telling a caller that the hotel was full just because there were no seats in the dining room. If they wanted to come just for an expensive dinner and a show that night they were always welcome. At times, the number of these D.O.s would bring the head count in the dining room to over 450. My first July 4th weekend, July of 1966, was one of those times.

Now a slightly experienced busboy, I was assigned for the summer to an experienced waiter named Robert Lewis. People called him Bobaloo, nicknamed I assumed either after a New York disk jockey named Bob Lewis, known on the radio as Bobaloo, or perhaps after Ricky Ricardo. Mrs. T. accepted close to 100 D.O.s that Saturday night. This meant that the dining room was seriously over capacity. The place was packed. There was no room to move between tables. I figured that if the hotel could get high school students released early to work there when it needed them, the Teitelmans must have worked out something with the Connecticut Fire Marshal as well.

When there were a full complement of guests and that many D.O.s, numerous problems arose. The kosher requirement of separate meat and dairy dishes and separate meat and dairy silverware became impossible to comply with. There were not enough for all the extra guests, if we were expected to use meat dishes and meat silverware only, at a meat meal. Nor were there enough tables, chairs, tablecloths, linen napkins, glasses, water pitchers, ashtrays, waiters or busboys for all these hungry people. Making matters worse was that we were supposed to set two forks, two knives and two teaspoons at each place, as the hotel considered itself to be classy. This was called "double setting." Since not having silverware for your guests to eat with was said to adversely affect your tips, waiters and busboys were forced to set some tables with single silverware.

Many waiters took to keeping the silverware drawers in their serving stations padlocked. They went to the hardware store in Stanbury, bought hasps and combination locks and installed them on their own. Some waited until just about the time guests were due to arrive before putting out the silverware, so their teaspoons were never left unguarded. This deep concern about protecting your silverware was not unfounded. It was not uncommon for my waiter, Bob, and me to leave the dining room at 3:30 p.m. with our tables all set for supper, having worked in the dining room continuously since 6:45 a.m., to return at 5:30 p.m. and find some of our double set tables now having only single silverware. Or, we might find the silverware missing entirely from several place settings or even from an entire table. Also not uncommon, was to find the hasp pried off and our silverware drawer broken into. Arguments commonly broke out between waiters over missing teaspoons.

Eventually I decided that when our silverware or our

few spares were not in use between meals, I'd keep them safe in the back parking lot, in the trunk of my Buick. Tables however, were another problem.

The Buick had an enormous trunk. Of necessity, I carried a large number of spare parts with me. My clothing, our meat and dairy silverware for 40, a spare tire, a spare carburetor, water pump, generator, starter motor, fan belts, radiator hoses, motor oil and gallons of water, left little room for folded tables in my trunk. So even if you had the linen and silverware for your extra guests, you still needed a table to put it on. If we did not use broken or very wobbly ones, there were not enough tables when the hotel dining room was so severely overbooked. Sometimes, when the hotel was busy, some of the busboys took turns guarding one another's stations during what was supposed to be our short periods of time off between meals; sort of a Neighborhood Teaspoon Watch in the dining room. Terrible things could happen on a busy weekend if your station was not guarded or you left your silverware in harm's way.

But on Saturday, July 3, 1966, the night before the holiday and before we decided to stand guard in the afternoons or consistently use my Buick as an anti-theft device, Bob and I returned at 5:30 p.m. only to find a big empty space in the dining room where one of our completely set tables for eight used to be. Apparently, a waiter in need of another table and chairs and the silverware to go with it, had simply stolen the entire table, linen, glasses, dishes, silverware, chairs and all. Since the waiter who took our table would have rearranged the tables at his station so that his extra table appeared to belong there, identifying our table from among almost fifty other identical ones in a highly overcrowded dining room was virtually impossible.

Some waiters, including Bob, had long ago taken to putting secret pencil marks on the underside of their tables to help identify them later in case of a dispute. One used a permanent marker on his tables with part of his social security number. When our table "disappeared," Bobaloo began crawling around the dining room floor on all fours raising tablecloths, in an effort to find the pencil marks that would prove a table was his. He was not successful. Obviously, when we lost a table this way we inevitably lost a lot of our silverware. With guests due in the dining shortly, Bob was angry. I wondered how we would tell our hotel guests that there was nowhere for them to sit and have dinner, because someone had stolen their table. Bob got a wobbly table from the basement. We reduced one of our tables to single settings and we single set our wobbly table. We were back in business, just before our guests arrived.

Being a waiter for the last three years, Bob had experienced this before. That explained why he had already begun to encourage me to systematically pilfer silverware from neighboring waiters and their tables. I was to take a spoon here, a fork there when I walked past a place setting with no one seated yet or no one looking, in anticipation of the busier weekends of the summer. I could store these "spares" in my Buick for safekeeping. He told me not to think of what I was doing as stealing. "That wasn't what it was", he explained. "We were just saving up for Labor Day," another predictable major D.O. overbooking disaster in the dining room.

When the hotel was that much over capacity, there were other issues as well. Each waiter was assigned too many people. To make matters worse, the D.O.s did not necessarily arrive at post time like the hotel's guests. They dribbled in, since they had to stop at the Main House and pay for the event before being sent along to the dining room. That meant we would be serving some guests appetizers while others were getting their main course. It meant we were hanging from the moment we started.

My first full season at the hotel, the captain was a law student and the maître d' a business major. The maître d', or "Major Dean," as one elderly European woman called him, was Joe Mayr. Joe was a bit older than the rest of us and always impeccably dressed. A handsome guy with black, wavy hair, he always had a cigarette going and was generally drunk at dinnertime. Our captain of the waiters, Michael Sheffield, the law student, was from Vermont and driving an Alfa with Tennessee license plates. It seemed that Michael had a girlfriend in Tennessee, providing him an opportunity to register his car more cheaply and in a state that did not require him to carry auto insurance. Clearly, he was destined to be a great lawyer. Michael also always had a cigarette in his mouth, or more accurately hanging from his lower lip. His girlfriend, a sweet and very pretty slightly heavy redhead named Debbie Jo Walker, worked as a counselor at the hotel's day camp that summer. Michael got her the job. But Michael did not pay enough attention to her, preferring to pursue married female guests at the hotel much of the time. Debbie, being far from home and lonely, became very friendly with several of the waiters, those brave enough to chance Michael finding out. Often, very late at night, you could see a small light on, up on the hill in the otherwise dark day camp.

Michael and Joe were old buddies. For a time that summer they had an apartment together in the neighboring town of Stanbury. There were very few apartment complexes in the area in those days, but these guys managed to rent an apartment in one, just for the summer. The 30 or so apartments in this complex were all within a long, one-story building set up in a U-shape around a grass common, and facing the road. It looked a bit like a motel. Early that summer Michael and

Joe were evicted, however, as a result of their bodybuilding technique. At 11:45 a.m. on a Sunday morning, after breakfast at the hotel and while the other occupants of the apartment complex and their children were returning from church, Michael was on the common lifting weights in his jockey shorts. Joe was in boxer shorts.

Michael was interesting. Not much rattled him, even when he was arrested. The local constable in Kirby, Jim Ogorek, pulled Michael over one day on the Stanbury Road for speeding plus some question about his license and expired Tennessee registration. Jim then attempted to take Michael to the state police barracks in town. Even though this rural community valued the hotel, (the movie theatre in Stanbury was even known to hold the start time of a movie when waiting for a few hotel guests to arrive) Michael's behavior, both driving and verbal toward Constable Ogorek, overrode his status as the hotel's captain of waiters and the constable's usual deference to the hotel. Michael just never gave up. When the constable took his license and registration and instructed Michael to follow him to the police barracks in Stanbury, Michael did so, never exceeding 5 MPH the entire trip. Martin Teitelman had to bail Michael out.

Although Michael and Joe seemed to like me, they had assigned me to Bobaloo. He was not very well liked by anybody. While he was bright, a senior in college and predominately a nice guy, he had two serious flaws; a high pitched voice and he took this waiter business seriously. Because he was a much better waiter than Sal, more skilled and more organized, he expected me to actually follow the rules, most of the time. That was a problem for me, since I never was good at following rules at home growing up and Sal had taught me to violate them on an as-needed basis at the hotel. But even Bob was forced to make exceptions.

One Saturday evening, ten minutes after most guests had arrived and the dining room filled solid, Joe Mayr informed Bob that he was to set up another table for eight people coming for dinner, who were on their way over from the front desk; more of Mrs. T.'s D.O.s. Imagine being a waiter who has 32 people to serve, all of whom just sat down at once at four different tables. You have to serve them a choice of appetizer, soup, main course and dessert and you are not allowed to write their selections down. To give the appearance of class, all orders have to be stored in the waiter's head, never on paper. The line in the kitchen is 11 waiters long and moves slowly. Although you are serving 32 people, you are prohibited from taking more than 16 appetizers, 24 soups or 13 main dishes from the kitchen at any one time. These restrictions were based less on how much most waiters could carry than on management concerns about the amount of food wasted when a waiter fell or dropped his tray on the carpet. Bob was on his way out of the kitchen with our second tray full of appetizers when the maître d' told him to set up the additional table for eight dinner-only guests. After some angry whispering back and forth, Joe finally convinced Bob he was serious. I asked Joe where he would like us to get another table and table cloth, and if these people will mind not having silverware and standing while they ate. I heard one busboy shout "Set the chandelier for eight." Another voice from across the room suggested we "Set the phone booth for four."

Since there was no space in the dining room for another table even if we were sent one directly from the table factory, usually polite Bob asked the maître d' if he would mind if we seated these people nearby, in the Social Hall or at the pool. The maître d' responded by telling us to move our asses. At this point, Bob, an experienced waiter, knew exactly what to do. He delegated the problem to his busboy. Mouthing the words silently in this full dining room, I told him to "get fucked, it's impossible." But Bob could see that there was one solution. We would ask the guests at our four tables to stop eating their appetizers for a moment, then to stand, while we delicately slide their tables and chairs over, much closer together, making room for another table. Then we would steal a table.

Steven Dolinsky, another waiter, was standing in line in

the kitchen, sweating profusely, partly from heat and partly from high doses of alcohol. He was waiting to pick up a tray of appetizers and was panicky because one entire table of his did not come in at 7:00 as they were supposed to. He was worried about how he could get them caught up on their appetizers at the same time all of his other guests would be up to soup or their main dishes. His busboy was in the kitchen helping him. Steve's worrying had not been in vain. As a matter of fact, he had not worried enough, because as he came out of the kitchen carrying the appetizers, he noticed that his missing eight people had just entered the dining room and were on their way to an empty space where their table had once been. Bob and I were now just seating our eight D.O. guests at a fully set table he and I had carried overhead across a crowded dining room and placed in the corner of our station. When the argument broke out between Bob and Steve, I used the Nuremberg defense. Only the presence of hundreds of hotel guests prevented it from escalating into a fistfight. Steve and his busboy left their guests and headed for the basement in search of even a broken table. I avoided them both for several days, as their animosity toward us was very clear. Bob told me not to feel bad, as he had been told in confidence by an unnamed source that our stolen silverware on an earlier night had been the work of Steve and his busboy.

5
NEEDING FOOD TO STAY ALIVE

Competition for tables and silverware was tough, but it did not bring out my survival skills the way that getting enough food to stay alive did. Feeding over two dozen growing, hard-working waiters, busboys and bellhops ages 16 to 21 was very costly for the hotel and the Teitelmans tried hard to minimize the expense. Feeding us the livestock cultures left from yesterday was only part of their solution. Another was to give us food left over from the errors that the chefs made in predicting how many guests would order what and how much of each item to cook in advance. When feeding hundreds of people, most foods were prepared in advance. Even things like steak were cooked to the level of extremely rare just before the meal and placed on trays while waiting to be completed.

The menu always had a good selection but it was not uncommon for the kitchen to run out of one main course item and have a lot of another left over. In fact, there was a system to minimize the number of guests who could not get what they wanted at a given meal. As waiters began to come in with their orders, if it became clear that the chef had not projected well, waiters who had not yet taken all of their main dish orders would be told to discourage the item we were running out of and push the other items. That meant telling people that what you knew was good was bad, and what you knew was bad was good. The residual errors were what the staff got to eat, not including steak or roast beef, but only eventually. It might not have been so bad if we got leftovers at the next meal or the next day. Leftover chicken could be okay. But the chefs had the habit of freezing whatever was left over and giving it to us one to two weeks later. Hamburgers, chicken or fish cooked, left unwrapped, put on open trays and then frozen ten days prior was not very appetizing when reheated. Even breakfast was difficult for me. All of the cold cereals were available to us and you could toast the stale bread, but the milk was usually somewhat sour. It was livestock milk that had sat out on the tables for hours and then been returned to the kitchen. I liked to think of it not as old milk, but as early cheese. Fearful we would get scurvy by Labor Day, we organized, approached Martin and demanded orange juice with breakfast. What we got in response was concentrated water with orange juice flavor added.

Beyond my revulsion to meatloaf, I was becoming progressively more vegetarian in those days. In part, it was because of the gruesome sights below the kitchen in the butcher shop. I had to walk near the butcher shop to get to the Staff House by the most direct route. Half a dead steer hanging on chains and bleeding on the floor was the kind of sight that turned me vegetarian. The making of chopped liver, involving the cooking and grinding of hundreds of calves livers on a 95 degree summer day in a 105 degree kitchen produced an aroma that made me gag. I would hold my breath and look the other way as I passed this sight in the afternoon on my way through the kitchen. The net result was that I started my first summer at the Teitelman's Inn quite thin and then lost 20 lbs. My dinners consisted generally of ketchup sandwiches, coleslaw sandwiches, boiled potatoes, an overcooked vegetable and iced tea. Soon I was forced to delete coleslaw from my menu having seen the salad man make it.

During my first summer at the hotel, the salad man was a little guy named Al Sternberg. Al was about 60, grey and hairy, gruff, always needing a shave, and always with a cigar in his mouth, even while preparing food. His domain included all the cheese, butter, milk, cream, bread, juices and fruits, and he made all of the cold salads including tuna salad and egg salad, cold appetizers and Jell-O. His pantry was a screened-in corner of the kitchen, on the left just as you entered. One day I observed him bare-chested in the hot kitchen, as he mixed coleslaw for 300 in a gigantic bowl. No spoons. His arms went in almost to the armpits. Watching the coleslaw falling from his arms and chest and dropping back into the bowl, I quit eating coleslaw sandwiches and switched exclusively to Heinz ketchup on rye bread, each time trying to find an unopened bread and an unopened ketchup bottle. Why didn't Connecticut have laws or a Health Department to regulate coleslaw production? Boys pulled out of school to work as busboys. Overcrowded dining rooms. Hairy coleslaw. Where was the state government when we needed it? After all, Connecticut was the first state to ratify the U.S. Constitution!

Eating real food or "guest food" as it was called was a privilege accorded only to very few employees besides the chefs. The maître d' and the captain of the dining room were of course among those employees. Mayr and Sheffield would sit with Martin at the famous Teitelman Family Table after the guests had gone, eating steak and French fries. I had eaten ketchup on rye. Some waiters ordered extra, both for themselves and their busboys, but it was very dangerous. If any of us were seen ordering extra guest food from the kitchen and consuming it ourselves, we would be fired. Martin knew how many guests each waiter had at his station and he sometimes watched a waiter to see how many main dishes he ordered from the chefs. Since busboys generally did not order from the chef, but only handled exchanges, the difficulty in obtaining adequate food partly explained the high busboy turnover rate. I often had to demand that Bobaloo order extra. Since busboys did not make a lot of money each week in the summer, unlike the Christmas holiday week, most of us resented having to drive to town and spend our college tuition money on food, while the hotel claimed to provide us with "room and board" in lieu of a fair salary. So we developed certain methods of procurement.

One popular method was to eat guest food in the middle of a crowded, chaotic dining room, right in front of everyone, simply by swallowing rapidly with minimal, if any chewing. Many a muffin went down my throat like a snake eating a rodent. When I could convince Bob to order more food than we had guests, we stashed the extra in our serving station, so I could stuff huge pieces down unchewed when I thought no one was looking. Busboys assigned to stations along the window would actually take a piece of food and step behind the heavy floor-to-ceiling drapes and dare to chew. You just had to be lucky and not be seen going in or out from behind the drapes. There could be only one reason you were there. Your guests, of course, would wonder what the hell you were doing.

Martin and the maître d' would occasionally cruise the dining room looking into each waiter's serving station for food hidden on the upper inside shelf. If we saw them coming, the food would be crushed and dumped into the bus box. Management got very angry if we were seen eating in front of guests. Besides the fact that what we ate cost the hotel money, they did not want hotel guests to know we were being starved. They thought it detracted from the hotel's classy image. It never dawned on the Teitelmans that the mere presence of more than two dozen teenage waiters and busboys would in and of itself prevent the place from ever being classy.

Another alternative was to order extra food and never leave the kitchen with it. I would go to the back of the kitchen near the pot washers, where no one went because the smell was so bad, and swallow food unchewed while trying not to breathe. This too had its dangers, both because Martin often came back there looking, and because Henry Heimlich had not yet invented his maneuver. Always thinking about the waiters and busboys, the Teitelmans eventually put a stop to our eating in the back of the kitchen by installing closed-circuit TV cameras. Mrs. T. could now monitor the kitchen's dark corners from her office in the Main House.

A safer method of avoiding starvation was to make friends with the chefs, the salad man or the baker. Rule out the salad man. You could not get fired for eating food given to you by one of those people, but you had to eat it discreetly, in the kitchen. If you were accused by Martin, you could call the chef or baker as a witness on your behalf to testify that he had given you the food with the understanding that you were going to eat it yourself, not serve it. Only then would you be exonerated. If the chef gave it to you, it was okay. Even Martin was afraid of the chef, probably afraid he would quit in the middle of the season. The pantry man never liked me, but the new Chinese head chef who replaced Sal's father began to. This new chef, named Shing Chen, had no car and he spoke very little English, but his hair grew rapidly and he liked to get it cut frequently. By using sign language to volunteer to drive him to the barber in town once in a while during my precious couple of hours off, I occasionally was given some guest food as a reward. "*Good* busboy."

Once, when Martin caught me in the back of the kitchen with food I had "stolen," I claimed Shing Chen had given it to me. When Martin attempted to question Shing Chen about where I got the food, I spoke up and questioned Shing Chen myself. Shing Chen saved me. I was never sure that he understood the questions when he testified, so I phrased them so "yes" was the correct answer. My goal was to keep Shing Chen saying "yes," smiling and shaking his head up and down. So I'd say, "Shing Chen, you gave me this for myself, didn't you?" while shaking my head up and down. Martin assumed Shing Chen was actually saying "yes" when he shook his head. Perhaps I underestimated Shing Chen. He may have known what he was doing when he saved me.

I also made friends with our Hungarian baker, Vilmos Szabados, aka "Vil the Bake." Vil was about 70, had been a baker all of his life and had been at this hotel for about a decade. Vil made all of the pastries. He knew the boys were hungry. He soon learned my preferences and more often than not when I stopped in the bakery to say hello, he knew I was not really there to socialize. He was a nice man. He usually had a piece of apple cobbler in the back of his refrigerator waiting just for me. When I visited Vil, I always had a spoon in my pocket, just in case. I loved his apple cobbler. Inside the bakery, I was allowed to chew before I swallowed.

Telling the Jewish mother types among your guests that you were very hungry also worked well at getting you food. You could encourage them to order extra food, ask for a doggy bag to take with them after the meal, only to meet you later at a prearranged time and place to give you the food. I relied on this method as well during my first summer at the Teitelman's Inn. This approach was also said to improve your tips, as it made the Jewish mothers feel sorry for you.

All of these methods were spotty, however. I could not hit on Vil the Bake every day, Shing Chen only got a haircut every couple of weeks, and you had to be very careful about asking guests to get extra food for you. It was really dangerous. In the interest of helping you, they might take it upon themselves to ball out the Teitelmans for not feeding us enough. You would be in a lot of trouble when they left. Remember the hotel's classy image. The most successful method was always theft, especially at night, by getting into the kitchen during the nightly Tea Room between rounds of the night watchman. Management tried to deal with this problem by keeping the kitchen locked up like Fort Knox as much as possible.

Since many of the waiters and busboys were college students with high IQs, we developed ingenious methods of procuring food. Not even raccoons were better at it. Although the kitchen was locked up at night, the pantry and several of the walk-in refrigerators were unlocked from 10:30 p.m. to around midnight. This allowed the bellhops to serve coffee and cake to the guests at the nightly Tea Room after whatever show or event went on that night in the Social Hall. The guests could work up quite an appetite playing Bingo.

The waiters and busboys did not have primary responsibility for the Tea Room because we started work before 7:00 a.m. each day and worked seven days per week. Although the Teitelmans did not think we needed food, they did acknowledge that we slept once in a while. So the bellhops ran the nightly Tea Room, with each waiter and busboy assigned to help them only two or three times per week, as needed, on a rotating basis. This unpaid side job was known not surprisingly as Tea Room. Although there was no tipping at Tea Room, it did create an opportunity to try to serve your own guests. Since my waiter wasn't necessarily present, it gave me a chance to kibitz with my own guests in an effort to improve the tip they gave at the end of their stay. Prior to Tea Room, Martin or the night watchman opened the refrigerators and panty for the bellhops, thereby creating a potential opportunity for the waiters and busboys. Never clear to me was why the Teitelmans trusted the bellhops in the unlocked kitchen. They, too, were hungry teenagers. Perhaps it was because there were only a few of them. How much could they eat? But Martin frequently patrolled during Tea Room.

The giant walk-in refrigerator on the right in the kitchen just beyond the bread table contained a variety of ready to eat foods like cottage cheese, orange juice, Jell-O, fruit salad, smoked salmon, pickled herring and cases of fresh fruit. One of my most successful approaches was to enter the giant walk-in when no one was looking, close the door behind me, and cautiously exit some five or six minutes later quite full. I ate right out of the food containers. Usually I took a spoon in with me but sometimes an opportunity just presented itself when no silverware was handy. Often we would take turns in the refrigerator while one of us kept a lookout for Martin or the watchman and to make certain no one got locked in. The bellhops, although not as hungry as we were because of their legal nightly access to the kitchen, tended to look the other way when we ate. They only got irritated when we took advantage of the opportunity by carrying crates of melons out to our cars. Management interrogated the bellhops the next day, after finding dozens of cantaloupe carcasses on the ground outside the Staff House. The bellhops, of course, denied being complicit.

At other times, very late at night when the pantry was locked, the kitchen was dark and the only one around was the night watchman doing his rounds, we had another system. The kitchen ceiling was very high; 15 to 20 feet. In one corner of the kitchen was a locked 10' X 15' screened-in cage with wire mesh walls about 10 feet high. It had a screen door that was padlocked. That was the salad man's pantry. In addition to keeping his canned goods there, it's where Al Sternberg made the fruit salad, potato salad, tuna salad, egg salad and coleslaw. What he didn't store in the large walk-in refrigerator, was in a large free-standing one within his pantry. Willy from the Staff House was his assistant.

One of the waiters, Scott Katz, was quite agile. He was a little fellow with long fingers and long arms. We suspected simian ancestry because he could easily climb up the wire mesh wall, go over the top and down the other side into the cage. Once in the pantry, he would open the unlocked refrigerator. There he would often find a stainless steel pan about 2' X 2' X 1' full of freshly prepared tuna fish salad for the guests' lunch tomorrow. Someone would toss Scott a loaf of bread and a box of aluminum foil over the fence. Scott would begin making sandwiches, while we listened for the watchman. Working as fast as possible, Scott would remove the waxed paper cover from this pan of nicely smoothed tuna salad for a few hundred people. Using his hand as a scoop, he slammed tuna salad between two pieces of bread, quickly wrapped it in aluminum foil and tossed it over the top of the cage like a Frisbee. We would catch the flying sandwiches as they landed. We continued until either Scott or one of us panicked, or we thought we heard the watchman. We always left in a hurry.

I do not think it was so much the missing quantity of tuna that miserable, cigar-smoking Al Sternberg noticed the next day as readily as he noticed the dents in the mountain of tuna salad and the missing waxed paper cover. Al could never be absolutely sure if it was us or management that got into his tuna salad. He'd made remarks to us the next day about the tuna salad as if hoping someone would confess. We seemed to always get away with it. He certainly would not question the Teitelmans to see if they were in the tuna. More than likely this, plus the disorganized state we created in the big walk-in refrigerator, explained why Al was always nasty to the busboys and waiters and almost never gave us anything to eat. It amazed me how a salad man could give a waiter or busboy a hard time. Consider what happens when one of the people you are serving lunch to wants the Hawaiian fruit salad plate on the menu, but wants to substitute diet cottage cheese for the regular and wants only the red Jell-O, no green. Waiters got called a lot of names by Al, in English.

In an effort to revenge his tuna salad, Al decided one night to prepare some specially for the tuna pirates he was expecting. The tuna salad must have contained large quantities of laxative or bad mayonnaise, because all of the boys who ate tuna salad that night had diarrhea the next day. By sheer luck, I had gone to my aunt's house that night and was not part of that tuna raiding party. The sporadic midnight pantry raids continued, but egg salad increased in popularity for a time.

In an escalating series of reciprocal kindnesses, the group made ill by Al's tuna wanted revenge. Among the salad man's duties was the making of juice for our 350 or so breakfast guests. He would prepare giant vats of orange juice and grapefruit juice from quarts of frozen concentrate. The orange juice was prepared in a vat about 2' in diameter and 3' deep. Glasses were filled from it using a ladle. Tomato, and of course prune juice, the great favorite, were sourced directly from cans. In retaliation for the tuna laxative, a group of five took turns in the giant walk-in refrigerator one night during Tea Room, urinating in the orange juice. I refused to participate. The next morning, those of us that were aware of what had happened tried very hard not to be too obvious as we attempted to convince our guests that tomato juice was much better for them that morning. I went so far as to tell people that the orange juice delivery truck had broken down and the only OJ we had was a bit old.

6
ON BEING A BUSBOY

Over that first summer at the Teitelman's Inn I, like every other busboy, was forced to develop varied skills. Besides hunting for and gathering food, other skills related to saving time and conserving energy were critical. Acquiring them was like Natural Selection, since busboys who didn't became extinct by mid-July.

At breakfast and lunch each day the guests could choose from regular milk, skim milk and buttermilk, the latter being very popular. I never really understood why adults drank so much milk. We are the only species on the Earth that continues to drink the stuff beyond childhood and into adulthood and we don't even drink our own milk. Nevertheless, when a busboy went into the kitchen and poured say, six regular milk, three skim and five buttermilk, he would be careful to note their relative locations on his tray. If distracted between the kitchen and his station in the dining room, however, it was not unheard of to forget which milk was which. Or if you put your tray down in a different orientation than how you placed the milk while in the kitchen, confusion about which milk was which was easy. You could pick up a glass and slosh the milk around a bit trying to determine which was which, but it was hard to be certain. That's when I learned the advanced viscosity test. One of the other busboys showed me how to use my index finger, inserted deep into each glass and then withdrawn quickly, to measure the drip rate and determine which was buttermilk and which was skim. The thicker the liquid, the more slowly it would drip off your finger. Sometimes you had to go back and forth between the glasses comparing the drip rates repeatedly, since the differences were small. You had to do this quickly and without anyone in the dining room seeing you do it. Some of us got good at it.

The concept of viscosity also came in handy if you were short a skim milk. You solved that problem simply with the right mix of whole milk and water rather than make a trip back to the kitchen. I often suspected that the pantry staff "manufactured" skim milk this way whenever the hotel was running low. A somewhat related process was used for making orange juice when you came back from the kitchen short one or a guest dared to ask for a second. You simply waited until most of the people had finished their orange juices, collected their glasses and combined the residual from the bottom of say, ten used glasses, adding water as needed. Instant OJ.

When a guest complained that the meat was not well done enough, the busboy was sent to make an exchange. Not only did this waste valuable time, but the chefs were never happy about it. They were never sure if the guest was actually dissatisfied or if the waiter had screwed up the order. When my waiter sent me to make an exchange, a recommendation from more experienced busboys was not to actually do so. Since blood rose to the top of a piece of meat left standing, one of the other busboys taught me that well done was just a state of mind. If a guest asked for his steak or roast beef to be made more well done, you could turn your back and lean into the serving station, appearing to exchange the steak for another. In reality there was no other steak in there. You could simply use the rag you had hanging out of your back pants pocket, your side towel, and blot up the juices on, under and around the steak and flip it over. Voila, medium well. Also in the name of satisfying our guests, I learned the interchangeability of cooked cereals. The hotel had only oatmeal, cream of wheat and Wheatena. Anything requested other than these was given an equivalent color substitute and the waiter insisted that he had served the correct cereal.

Despite everything busboys knew about making the job easier, or perhaps because of it, by late July of my first season at the hotel, the busboy turnover rate was almost 50%. Many of the fellows I worked with just could not put up with the labor, the way we were treated, the Staff House and the poor food they served us. The proximity to a girl I had met at the hotel earlier that summer, living only a couple of hours away in Rhode Island, plus the prospect of becoming a waiter some day kept me going. Experienced waiters, I was told, made a lot of money.

The hotel got away with paying us a salary of $50 per month by convincing the State of Connecticut that we exceeded the required minimum hourly wage through the tips we received. Then the hotel charged us for room and board, subtracting it from the $50 per month and leaving us about $30 in salary for the entire summer. Not being treated as well as the local farm animals could be very hard on your self-esteem. The weight loss that resulted from hard labor and food deprivation did not help much either. We worked very long days after which we were assigned to help the bellhops at Tea Room two or three nights each week.

We also had another unpaid assignment two to three nights per week. It required that after you got out of the dining room at around 9:30 p.m., having begun by 7:00 a.m. that morning, you had to get cleaned up, dressed up and appear in the Social Hall to mingle with the hotel guests. The hotel's purpose in this assignment was certainly not to improve our social lives by requiring us to mingle with the teenage girls. We would have done that anyway, but not in the Social Hall. That was why I had a Buick. We were assigned there in order to lower the average age in the room and even to ask the older, single women to dance. We called this "Gigolo Duty." If I was observed spending too much time with the young ladies my age, I was told to mingle more with the older guests. It might have been good for my tips, but I resisted this assignment fiercely, avoiding compliance as much as I thought I could get away with. If you have blue hair, I won't dance with you. Sometimes when stuck in the Social Hall during the evening "entertainment," I wondered which I was most motivated to escape from, the blue hair or the awful entertainment that catered to the blue hair. The MC, the singer and the comedian were often one in the same individual. My music was Bob Dylan, Richie Havens, The Lovin' Spoonful and The Byrds, not The Andrews Sisters, Tex Beneke or The Modernaires.

Normally, the only other reason you would find me in the Social Hall was the canteen. A walled-off corner of the room and run by a nice couple who I assumed rented the space from the Teitelmans, it was the only source of food other than what we could steal during meals or from the kitchen, unless we drove to town. They sold soda, ice cream, candy, chips, cigarettes, newspapers, comics, etc. and even made some limited types of sandwiches. But of course, it cost money. Rich and Mookie, the couple that ran the place, allowed some of us to run up a tab there, expecting the bill to be paid each Sunday after we received our tips. This clearly 'ate' into my income as it did many of the busboys. There was a juke box located near the canteen that seemed to always be playing "Crystal Blue Persuasion," by Tommy James and the Shondells. To this day, when I hear that song, I'm transported to Teitelman's Social Hall.

Again thanks to Connecticut's progressive laws, hotels were permitted to work waiters and busboys seven days per week. My first summer, I worked from Memorial Day to Labor Day without a day off. At minimum, I was in the dining room from 7 to 11:30 a.m., 12:00 to 3:30 p.m. and 5:30 to 9:30 p.m., plus the two to three evenings per week I was assigned to Tea Room and the two to three to Gigolo Duty. Sometimes they were the same night. Also, every week came a rotation through a newly assigned side job, another name for forced labor. The side job could take a good chunk out of the 3:30 to 5:30 break I needed to physically recover. That job could be bringing up heavy bags of linen and sorting and shelving them. Known surprisingly as "linen room," it had you stuck in the hot linen room stacking piles of tablecloths and napkins or bagging dirty linen to be sent out to the laundry.

Another job that could be yours for a week was called "chef's dishes." It required moving hundreds of main dishes from the dishwasher area into the long, steam-heated cabinets below the stainless steel counters where the chefs plated the food. That allowed the chefs to serve food onto warm plates. The dishes were heavy, the kitchen was hot and the cabinets even hotter. Plus, I certainly did not want to be in the kitchen if they were making chopped liver.

Overall, including Tea Room and side jobs, I averaged almost 14 hours per day labor that first summer, seven days per week. Gigolo duty, not officially considered work by hotel management, is not included in that estimate. The Social Hall adjoined the dining room, which of course adjoined the kitchen. Therefore, "Gig" duty did have the advantage of providing an explanation for why I was hanging around the dining room at 11:00 p.m. on a night I was not serving tea. It aroused less suspicion while I conspired to get into the kitchen.

Among the other tasks sometimes assigned to me for which I did not get paid, was being the bread delivery boy. The hotel got all of its bread from the Stanbury Bakery. Three-hundred and fifty guests plus waiters and busboys could eat a lot of bread. They did let us eat bread, although generally it was old bread. Our own baker, Vil, handled only the pastry. The bakery did not deliver, however. Someone had to take the hotel station wagon to town and pick up all of the bread the guests might eat in the next 24-48 hours. Martin would commandeer one of us and send us to Stanbury for the bread. He would pull me out of setting my tables for the upcoming meal, even when the guests were due in 20 minutes. He'd toss me the keys to the baby blue '65 Chevy wagon and tell me to pick up the bread.

Normal travel time for the four miles from the hotel to the Stanbury Bakery was eight or nine minutes. So of the 20 minutes until I needed to be with my waiter as our guests arrived, 16-18 would be on the road. That left only two to four minutes to load the station wagon with bread for 350 and then unload it back at the hotel. I had to cut the travel time to make it work. Martin did this to me often. It turns out that the hotel's '65 Chevy wagon had a safety defect that in 1971 resulted in General Motors recalling about 6.6 million cars. Although GM refused to admit that the vehicles contained a safety defect, there were many deaths due to what was later described as "sudden acceleration caused by broken motor mounts." Unbeknown to those of us driving the breadmobile, we had one of those vehicles. It wasn't 1971 yet and no one knew (except GM).

Not to switch into Auto Mechanics 101, here was the problem. If you look at a running engine from the front of the car, you will see that the fan is rotating clockwise. So are the internal parts of the engine. As we learned from Isaac Newton, every action has an equal and opposite reaction. Therefore, with the engine internals rotating clockwise, the engine itself wants to rotate counterclockwise. If you look under your hood while someone guns your engine, you will see the engine lift and rotate counterclockwise just a bit, each time they hit the gas. But the engine is mounted to the frame such that it can't go very far. The mounting is done on rubber blocks, called motor mounts, attached to both the motor and the frame it sits on. Their purpose is to hold the engine in place while dampening vibration from the engine, keeping it from being passed through to the frame and body of the car. The rubber is molded with threaded bolts sticking out to allow securing it down. Each time you accelerate, and the engine tries to rotate counterclockwise, it stresses the rubber motor mount on the driver's side, the side that is trying to lift. If that mount's rubber tears, under acceleration the engine will actually lift up off the frame on that side and rotate, enough to dent the hood from the underside and even tear into the shroud around the fan with the spinning blades. But that's not the big problem. In most cars of that era, the connection from the gas pedal to the carburetor was a long rod that came through a hole in the firewall (the wall between the engine and the dashboard). That hole was small, as the rod normally just moved forward and back through it. If under hard acceleration the driver's side of the engine lifted, that rod, called the "throttle linkage," lifted and became jammed against the top of the hole it passed through. That prevented the gas pedal from coming back up even when you took your foot off. So if the motor mount broke, once you accelerated and the engine lifted, the car continued to accelerate even if you came off the gas. Unless you were quick enough to turn off the engine or put the car into neutral, the engine would not sit back down and release the gas pedal. It would not come back up and the car would just keep accelerating. Even hard application of the brakes, most drivers' first instinct, would not overcome the acceleration. Hence dead drivers.

The Chevy wagon was always parked behind the kitchen. A long gravel driveway got you out of the hotel property from behind the kitchen straight toward Route 305 where you had to turn left or right; right if you were heading to the bakery. Straight across the road if you did not go left or right was Lake Gilmer. One of the days Martin picked me to get the bread over my strenuous objection, I took off in the wagon. I peeled out at the speed of light in a cloud of dust and a Hi Yo Silver heading for Route 305. When I took my foot off the gas the wagon kept going, flying ever faster toward cross traffic on 305. I was approaching 40 MPH. If no collision occurred there, I'd be launched into the lake. Fortunately, my interest in cars and my growing skills as a mechanic saved my life. I got the wagon into neutral, which let the engine sit down and free the gas pedal. I slammed on the brakes just in time to stop about five feet beyond the intersection, fortunately, with no cars coming. From that point on, no hard acceleration with the station wagon. I was late getting back to the dining room. Our guests had already been seated and my waiter was frantic. I caused us to hang that meal.

Years later, I learned that a teacher in the elementary school I had attended in the Bronx was killed under similar circumstances. No, she was not a busboy and she was not picking up bread. She experienced the same type of motor mount failure but in a 1960 Buick Special.

Another unpaid job duty that was almost exclusively mine was that of hotel tailor. When a busboy bent down to slide an overloaded bus box out of the server and onto his shoulder, not an uncommon occurrence was a major tear in his seat seam. Working in the dining room with your white jockey shorts showing out the back of your tuxedo pants was probably not good for your tips, even if you were not embarrassed. It seemed I was the only boy in the dining room who could sew. My parents were in the dry cleaning business in New York and machinery always fascinated me. So in addition to auto mechanics, I loved to play with the sewing machines, eventually developing a tiny bit of skill. Not infrequently I was in the bathroom hand sewing a sloppy backstitch to reassemble a busboy's pants while he stood in his jockeys loudly pleading with me to hurry up. In the meantime, my guests lived with their dirty dishes and waited for coffee. Generally, I was able to counterbalance their displeasure with their laughter when I told them I had been busy in the bathroom sewing up somebody's pants.

Preferring to do work that I actually got tipped for, Sunday afternoons if I did get a couple of hours out of the dining room in the late afternoon, I usually volunteered as an extra bellhop. As there were not enough bellhops to help all of the guests, they welcomed my offer to assist in carrying luggage for the guests who were checking in or out. It was possible to make an extra $15-20 each Sunday as a bellhop. I tried to get the younger people who were checking in or out. They tipped much better than the old people. It was awful when I carried two heavy suitcases up to the third floor of the Main House and was generously rewarded with 25 cents while being called "Sonny." I never understood what made the old people's suitcases that heavy. I suspected they were bringing there own cans of prunes and prune juice.

Usually, a busboy graduated to being a waiter if he survived a summer and returned for another season. The primary reason I survived that first summer was the girl in Rhode Island. Staying in Connecticut in July and August made it much easier to see her than it would have been had I given up and returned to New York. I did many overnight round trips to Rhode Island, departing the hotel at 9:30 p.m. and returning by 7:00 a.m. the next morning. Fortunately for teenage boys, sleep is rarely a priority. But still I frequently thought about quitting most of that first summer. When cleaning up or setting up you could often hear me singing a line from the Bob Dylan song "Just Like Tom Thumb's Blues" - "I'm going back to New York City, I do believe I've had enou..ou..ough." I didn't make much money either that first summer. Busboys were tipped separately by the guests usually at between 50% and 70% of what they gave the waiter. Bobaloo, my waiter that first summer, was a medium to low-station waiter. That meant he was assigned many of the older, less affluent guests. Some decent tippers but many not so generous ones. A waiter the bosses did not like did not make a lot of money. When the waiter made poor money, so did his busboy. Averaged across the summer, I made only $ 60-75 per week, including both tips and salary, after the hotel got away with charging us room and board and we paid a tiny bit of tax. I actually had to pay to sleep in the Staff House and for the toxins they gave us to eat. That was why I bellhopped on Sundays. Whenever I attempted to increase my tips by kibitzing with the guests, Bob, like Sal before him, admonished me not to be too friendly with them while he was in the kitchen getting food, or the guests might improperly split the tips more equitably between us. He did not want me cutting him either.

I noticed that almost all of the college-age waiters and busboys used a common system for increasing their tips. They told their guests that they were pre-med. The assumption was that if your guests thought you were going to medical school you would get a better tip than if you told them you were studying to be a gym teacher. So besides all of the D.O.s at the hotel, we had lots of soon-to-be M.D.s.

My 1955 Buick Super Convertible
Circa 1965 in the Bronx

7
THE BUICK

My 1955 Buick and the Teitelman's Inn were for me inextricably bound together. The way I saw it, I could not get to the hotel to make money if I didn't have the Buick and I couldn't keep the Buick on the road if I was not making money at the hotel. Plus, for some inexplicable reason, I loved driving the thing. While everyone else was in a '55, '56 or '57 Chevy, I drove around in a Buick!

Buicks and I had a long history. My father drove Buicks since I was a toddler. Though a product of the 1949 model year myself, I remember my dad's '50 Buick Super. It was two-toned; two variations on the ugliest green color imaginable. I remember sitting in my car seat in the front, between my parents, honking the red horn button on my little white steering wheel, driving my dad's new Buick. But it was the '55 Buick Super Riviera (a two-door hardtop) he bought a few years later that hooked me. I loved that car. He kept the blue and white beauty until late '63 and so it was the first car I ever sat behind the actual steering wheel of and the first car I ever attempted to repair or modify. Late one night in the Bronx it was hit. Some gentleman wearing shorts dropped a hot cigarette ash on his leg while driving and ran into my father's parked Buick.

Between that and problems with the Dynaflow transmission, the Buick's time was up. When it went to a junkyard in the Bronx, I was 14. It broke my heart. The following day, I led my two 11-year-old twin brothers on a long, unauthorized march from the West Bronx to the East Bronx, hoping to see our beloved Buick one last time. Upon arriving at the junkyard, we were horrified. Webster Auto Parts had cut the Buick in half across its width, just behind the front seat. The two big pieces were sitting in a stake body truck on Webster Avenue with half of another car, evidently destined to be melted. What a sight. A cut up '55 Buick and three young boys standing together on a busy, dirty, commercial street in the Bronx, crying over it, like babies.

The die was cast. I vowed to get a Buick of my own someday. Somehow, that would make up for the destruction of our father's '55. Although living in New York City required that you be 18 to drive, at age 14, I was now in search of a Buick of my own. It had to be a convertible of course.

Shortly after my 16th birthday, I spotted what looked like a 1955 Convertible Buick almost totally buried in snow during a March storm in the Bronx. When the sanitation department plowed the street they had relocated most of the snow onto this Buick. I dug through the snow and got the car's license plate number. A cop named Marty Lonegan, who was an acquaintance of my Dad's, got me the owner's name and phone number from the plate number. I called the man. He explained that the car did not run and was destined for the junkyard once the snow melted enough to dig it out. He was therefore reluctant to sell me the car and tried hard to discourage me. It was a white '55 Buick Super convertible with a red interior and 96,000 miles. I insisted on buying it and he finally agreed. He asked me for only $15, the same amount he'd likely get from the junkyard. It cost an additional $9 to have it towed home. I rented space for it in a private fenced-in parking lot near our apartment building for $12 per month. My parents were furious. Their brand new Buick Wildcat was parked on the New York City streets all night. My junkyard car had a private space in a fenced-in lot.

It took a long time to get the '55 running, with lots of parts purchased from that infamous junkyard. For a time, I drove it in New York City with no license plates and no driver's license. But that's a story for another day. Many months of working on it mechanically, then removing most chrome and repainting it using cans of dark gray primer to look like the '57 Chevy's of that era, and it was roadworthy. My first summer at the hotel, working as a busboy, I was old enough to take the Buick to Connecticut.

My parents assumed that the majority of the money I made at the hotel would go toward my NYU tuition. That was certainly my goal as well, except that like me, the Buick liked money. It wanted new tires, new upholstery, new cylinders to raise and lower the convertible roof and a repair to the radio. The radio repair was high priority.

The Buick had a tube radio of course, but one with features very unusual for 1955 manufacture. It had a signal-seeking function - like the scan button on modern radios. Instead of five buttons on the radio that you could preset to your five favorite AM stations, as was common in those days, it had one long black bar. It you touched the bar, the radio would begin looking for the next station on the dial and stop there. You could adjust the sensitivity of the radio, that is how many stations it stopped at, by turning a knob. It could stop at every station it found or only stronger ones. You could watch the red needle on the radio dial move all by itself, as it sought the next station. Buick called it a "Selectronic" radio. Really interesting was that not only could you send the radio into seeking the next available station by touching the bar, but it also had a button on the floor, to the left of the brake and right of the dimmer switch that would initiate seeking. A 1955 car and you could change the radio station without ever taking your hands off the wheel. How cool is that? But mine couldn't find any stations and would not stop seeking at all once the bar was pressed, and so I sought help from a Buick dealer only 20 minutes from the hotel, in the town of Tom's Ferry. They couldn't help, but directed me to man at the other end of town who could.

The gentleman they sent me to, although totally blind, was in the auto radio repair business. He had a young teenage son who would remove the radio from your car. He would put it on the bench, open it up and then his dad would go to work. His dad would hook up electricity to it and then would check for voltage in specific places, sometimes by having his son read from a meter he connected. But in addition to using a meter, he checked circuits by licking the end of his finger and probing around in the radio. I could not believe what I was seeing. A blind man was checking electrical current with a wet finger. The 12 volts from a car battery hurts. I knew that from personal experience. This man was a living voltmeter. When he found the problem, in my case a bad condenser, he snipped it out with a wire cutter, had his son read the value printed on the condenser and get him a new one. He then soldered in the new one with some limited help from his son and had his son cover anything he did with electrical tape. My radio was now working.

The Buick dealer in Tom's Ferry was managed by Mr.

Dolan. I knew that because his son was one of the busboys at the hotel. My '55 needed two new hydraulic cylinders to raise and lower the convertible top. Both of mine were leaking. The auto parts stores did not have them, as these were parts for a 11-year-old car. In those days, that was a rather old car. Mr. Dolan said they were no longer listed in his master parts book either, so that meant they were no longer available from General Motors. That was a problem for me. A convertible whose roof would not go up and down. Nice man that he was, Mr. Dolan had an idea. He said he had the old, outdated parts books upstairs in the attic. They had been updated and he was not supposed to order from them. Some parts had been discontinued and others had their part numbers revised. But he said he would find the old part numbers and place the order anyway, and we would see what happens. Two weeks later one hydraulic cylinder arrived. A week after that, another one. Wow. Just one side effect. Between the radio repair and new top cylinders, my college tuition was being pilfered away. The little money I was making at the hotel only stretched so far.

My mother hated my '55 Buick, but not because of its effects on my tuition money. She was convinced it was unsafe and unreliable. Years later, when we moved from the Bronx to a beautiful home in Westchester, she was not fond of seeing this chromeless grey beast sitting in her driveway. I often heard my car described as a "shitbox."

After Mr. Dolan came up with the hydraulic cylinders for me, I still needed another part to get the top working. The car had special high pressure rubber hoses that ran between the top's electric hydraulic pump and the cylinders that moved the roof. Buick did not have those either and again none of the auto parts stores did. Mine were rotten. Someone had told me about a mid-50's Buick convertible that looked like mine, sitting abandoned about eight miles from the hotel. Out of curiosity, two of my friends came along to help me search for it. We spotted the car. It was way off the road, deep in a field.

A big decision at this point. Was it legal to take parts off it? If this car was really abandoned, was it still theft? Being fine young men, we normally limited our stealing to things belonging to the Teitelmans. Was it safe? It was deep in really thick brush. Being teenagers, we decided to proceed. Weeds and a small tree were growing into the car through the floor that had rotted away. We trampled and tore out tall dense grass and brush as we labored to get the door open and struggled to climb in. We were watching for snakes. The hoses that supplied fluid the convertible top cylinders were located behind the back seat. The three of us managed to pull the back seat out. The hoses I needed were there and they appeared to be serviceable. With the wrenches I brought along we were able to remove them without tearing them. I also liberated a few other useful parts from this car's dashboard and interior and we left as fast as we could. I wanted to pull the radio out to have as a spare, but the rotted floor and concern about snakes dissuaded me from crawling under the dashboard. When we got back to the hotel, I thanked my peers for helping me, something they would never again agree to do. All three of us came down with poison ivy a few days after our Buick adventure. I had just a little on one arm. They were covered with it and worried that Martin might notice and not let them work. He was fussy that way when it came to our appearance. We were even subjected to fingernail inspections randomly and on Saturday nights before we served dinner. One of the other boys convinced them that the best thing for poison ivy was buttermilk. The poor boys believed him and could be seen applying buttermilk to their arms and ankles frequency over the next two weeks when Martin wasn't looking. I just tried hard not to scratch.

Gasoline and oil changes were available at the only gas station in Kirby. Close to the Kirby town green, was Walczak's Amoco. Mr. Walczak was an older man with white hair. He pumped the gas. His son, known to everyone as Walczak, was the mechanic. The gas station did not have a lift. Instead it had an inside pit - a huge rectangular cutout in the floor about 4' by 8' and about 7' deep with concrete walls and a concrete floor. At one end, the concrete formed a set of steep steps that would allow you to go down to the bottom. A large rolling canister in the pit could be positioned under a car to catch the oil being drained. In most old, rural gas stations that still had a pit rather than a hydraulic lift, someone would go down in and someone else would drive the car over it so it could be worked on from below. I went down in the pit once with Walczak and immediately felt like I had been buried alive. It was even more horrifying when he reached up and grabbed the suspension of my 4,500-pound Buick parked at one end of the pit and pulled the car over us. I'm not talking about pushing a 4,500-pound car. This was grabbing one while standing underneath it and pulling it over you. Now I was scared. If he died down here I could never get out of this pit. Last time I ever watched him do an oil change from below. These farm boys were sure strong. No wonder Hank sought them out as busboys.

Now it was time for new upholstery. Donahue's Auto Upholstery in Plain Ridge was the place. Frank Donahue was easy to deal with and a very skilled auto upholsterer. The Buick needed new seat upholstery and new door panels to match. I could not afford all of it at once so Frank made a section for me every few weeks. I'd zip over there during my break between lunch and dinner and he'd take measurements. Next time I came by, I'd wait while he'd install the item he made. First the front seat, then the door panels, then the rear seat. Each time I left I raced back to the hotel to set up for dinner. It took the entire summer to get the work done this way, but in the end, the Buick had pleated red vinyl seats with white stitching. I even got new red carpeting. At least in my view, "shitbox" had been removed from the license plate. At the end of the summer as a busboy, I went home with less money toward tuition, but beautiful seats.

8
BECOMING A WAITER

Approaching the end of my sophomore year at NYU, I faced a summer both needing a job and wanting to get out of the Bronx heat. The decision to return to Connecticut and hopefully become a waiter was a difficult one. Living arrangements and getting enough to eat were major concerns and even discounting the long, hard hours, I'd again have to deal with Martin Teitelman.

Martin's parents however, seemed like nicer people. At least I never had any real problems with them. By the end of my first summer, Mrs. T. was friendlier with me than the first day I met her. Edna was a little lady whose short, thinning hair was always in a tight permanent. She tried to keep it blonde, although you could always see serious shades of blue in it. Something about the Kirby water, I supposed. Morris Teitelman was a reasonable guy with the waiters and busboys. While I had begun to like him, I tried not to forget how he squeezed my uncle for a kickback of the commission on his insurance policies. Morris T. drank a lot on Sundays. When I bellhopped, it was not uncommon to spot him in the inner room of the front office drinking Scotch Whiskey straight out of the bottle along with the hotel's bandleader. Morris was not a bad looking older man, a kind of overweight cross between Claude Rains (the local police Captain Louis Renault in the movie Casablanca) and Groucho Marx. Like Groucho, he had a moustache and always had a cigar in his mouth. It made his already mumbled speech even harder to understand. The alcohol didn't help either. Two of the waiters did near perfect imitations of Morris T.'s voice that kept us laughing. One even called the hotel from a phone booth in town, asked for Martin and did a flawless imitation of Morris T. giving Martin instructions, before the waiter broke up laughing and had to hang up. Martin laughed a little but was too much of an ass to accept being the subject of a prank. He never did push to find out for certain who the caller was, but he knew there were only two boys who could imitate his father that well.

I thought about why I had not quit during the previous summer as a busboy, making little money and putting up with so much crap. But waiters who moved up in the ranks made a lot of money. And we did have fun. So I decided to return to Connecticut. I contacted the Teitelmans in April and was invited back. I returned to the hotel in mid-June and expected to become a waiter. After all, surviving a full summer as a busboy taught me a great deal and showed what I was made of. So many of the other busboys had quit. I had learned to get along with Martin, the chefs and salad man and made enough friends in the kitchen to avoid anorexia, scurvy and beriberi. I had learned many time-saving tricks, both appropriate and otherwise and survived the kitchen with all ten fingers. I knew what decent service looked like. I had learned not to serve food by passing it across people and to keep my eyes moving constantly across my tables. If someone needed something or was unhappy with their food, they were not to have to struggle to gain my attention. I learned that people do not like being served hot food cold or cold food warm. I was not to serve a beverage with my fingers placed around or near the rim of the glass, but always to hold a glass such that my fingers never touched where the person's mouth would. I had learned to carry a waiter's tray.

While many hotels and restaurants use covers over the plates as they come out from the kitchen, this hotel did not. Covers, of course, help keep the food hot and allow stacking of one plate directly on top of another. The Teitelman's Inn did it differently. No covers. Four main dishes went onto the tray. They just fit. Then four more were staggered in between those four but above them. Then a third story of four more dishes, again staggered, went on the top. A 13th dish went on the top, if the chef let you take more than 12, centered on this precarious mountain of food. Since we used no covers on the main dish plates, I had learned to rotate and position the lower dishes so as not to get food stuck to the underside of the plates above them. Never serve plates with mashed potato or gravy stuck to the bottom. The tray was carried on my left shoulder and balanced with only my left hand. I had gotten pretty good at it and even developed a new technique for avoiding collisions with guests or other waiters. Since saying "excuse me" or "coming through" never seemed to get anyone's attention, I'd yell "hot soup," even if I was carrying ice cream. It was amazing how fast people would jump to attention and get out of my way.

If a waiter or busboy did crash into someone, fell or was careless, dishes broke. The hotel had a great system for discouraging breakage. We had to pay a fine for anything we broke. Each type of dish had a set value. You had to "donate" the value of each dish you broke into a money pool. Separate pools for waiters and for busboys. At the end of the summer, the Teitelmans got to keep half the money in each pool; the other half went to the waiter and busboy who broke the least. The fines were not enough to pay for the dishes but they did create an incentive to be careful as well as an incentive to rat on any of your friends that broke a dish. In fact, when someone wiped out, the dining room became more like a high school cafeteria, with all of the boys rushing to the scene of the accident. Never mind serving your guests or getting on line in the kitchen; you wanted to make certain that the waiter or busboy was "credited" with the full extent of the damage and required to kick into the pool accordingly. My breakage rate was low, though I never won.

Besides having learned to carry a tray, I had improved at

carrying multiple items to a table at once. It was all about technique. Carrying multiple cups of coffee involved starting with two saucers "butterflied" in your fingers. You used your left hand. One saucer was placed with the right edge of the plate resting on your left pointer finger. Your thumb was on top of the saucer, just above your pointer. Doing that allowed you to keep the plate balanced. A second saucer would be placed to the right, just under the first one and slightly overlapping with it. It rested on your second finger and was supported from below by your ring finger and pinky. Cups of coffee could then be placed on the saucers. Since the rim in the center bottom of a saucer fit nicely into the top of a cup, you could repeat the butterfly with a second layer of cups and saucers. Now you were carrying four in your left hand. One more cup and saucer in the right hand and you were ready to run with five hot cups of coffee.

The process was similar but with a bit of modification for carrying appetizers or main dishes. Two dishes butterflied in your left hand, but then one underneath held up by your middle finger. Then you turned your wrist inward and put one more just above your wrist with the outer edge resting on the two that were butterflied. One more could be added higher on your arm, supported by the edge of the one on your wrist. And one higher on your forearm. Then, of course, one more in the right hand. Six plates of appetizers could thus be carried at once. If you had long and strong fingers you could do the same with main dish plates. But remember, you must not let food from a dish below transfer onto the bottom of a dish above. And it was hot food being placed onto pre-heated, heavy dishes. As I got good at all this, serving was faster and more efficient. I was ready to be a waiter that second summer, but the hotel was not ready for me.

No surprise, there was a shortage of busboys at the start of my second season, but more waiters than expected had returned. Normally, the hotel intentionally overstaffed the dining room at the beginning of the season due to the dropout rate along with the occasional firing. Two experienced waiters who were not at the hotel last summer had returned this year. Plus, the Teitelman's grandson, Paul, came up from Virginia to work as a waiter after having skipped the last several seasons. Martin needed me all right, but he had more than enough waiters. He saw me for what I was, the most highly skilled busboy at the hotel.

The assignment I was given was the privilege of continuing to be a busboy, but working for Richard Feiner, the new captain of the dining room. Michael Sheffield, last year's captain and Joe Mayr, the former major dean, had not returned this summer. They had been there for many years before me and had moved on. Martin hired a young blonde girl named Deana who he was clearly attracted to as the maître d' and promoted Richey Feiner to captain of the waiters.

Richey was a very experienced waiter who seemed easy to deal with. At least he served dinner sober. When Michael, our previous captain, served dinner on Saturday nights he was normally drunk. His busboy would follow behind him as he carried a tray with 13 main dishes and catch the ones that fell off the back of the tray as Michael waddled back and forth heading for his tables. Richey was never drunk during a meal. Now, as the captain's busboy, I had an interesting job. I did a lot of waiter work and was treated better in the kitchen than the other busboys, but still not as good as a waiter.

The captain, himself partly a waiter and partly the assistant manager of the dining room, reported directly to the maître d' and to Martin T. As such, he did not do the labor that the other waiters did. That labor was assigned to his busboy and to two other busboys assigned to help his, after they got their own work done. That was another of the side jobs a busboy would be assigned. It was called "Captain's Station." When a meal began, the Captain simply waltzed in, served the guests he had hand picked for his station and waltzed out. His busboy plus the two assigned to the captain's station did all of the setup and cleanup. The captain was allowed to eat guest food in public after the guests had left and could even sit at the table with the Teitelmans, if invited.

Since he had the wealthiest guests at his tables and got preferential treatment by the chefs, he gave great service and made much more money than anyone else. As his busboy I would make 50-70% of what Richey made, which would be more than any other busboy and even some of the waiters. Logically, I should have been happy with this assignment, but I wanted to be a waiter, not a busboy. I preferred to be low station waiter rather than high station busboy, but the 1967 season started off with me as the captain's busboy. Objection to not having been made a waiter got me nowhere. I simply hoped that if I was patient, perhaps one of the waiters would die, quit or get fired. It did not happen. But something else did.

Captain Richey had a new Volkswagen Beetle his parents bought for him. Late one night he and one of the other waiters decided to chase some girls they spotted driving in the other direction on a windy Connecticut back road not too far from the hotel. As he was somewhat intoxicated, it was no surprise that during a U-turn he made in pursuit of the girls, Richey backed into a tree and crushed a rear fender. He was really upset. He damaged his new Beetle, his parents would be angry, his insurance would go up and he never even caught up to the girls. Richey had a problem and we were all laughing about it.

Almost everyone at the hotel knew I was something of

an auto mechanic. If they did not know from previous conversations with me, they probably could tell from the appearance of my 1955 Convertible Buick Super. It clearly looked like a vehicle that had been saved from the junkyard, but made it here more than once, all the way from New York City. Only a good mechanic could have accomplished that. So in the middle of staff lunch two days after Richey Feiner's accident, Richey asked me in front of everyone if it was true that I could fix cars. I said "Yes, and I can also be a waiter." Richey bought a fender and I installed it. He had it painted for $20. The next Sunday I became a waiter. Low station waiter. In fact, they created an extra station for me right in front of the kitchen. It was almost in the kitchen. But I was a waiter and would remain a waiter.

This promotion of course was in title only. It immediately resulted in a large drop in my earnings. The hotel guests assigned to me were mostly the prune juice set who stayed in the Main House for the week on the second or third floors - the cheapest rooms in the hotel. The rooms were small, had no air conditioning and shared bathrooms at the ends of the hall. I was never sure how some of the guests actually made it up and down from their rooms.

During the summer season, most guests at the hotel came for a week. They checked in for supper on Sunday and stayed through lunch (called dinner) the following

Sunday, a total of 21 meals. Most were couples, although some people were alone. They were assigned permanent seats in the dining room and thus kept the same waiter and busboy. As described earlier, a group of tables in a given area was referred to as a waiter's station. Each station was defined by a number on the tables and a wooden cabinet, the server, along the isle. That was where you put down your tray and stored your silverware. The new station, the one created for me, was right next to the kitchen doors and right next to the Family Table. That was a problem.

The Teitelman's Family Table was like a feudal lord's castle. From there, they watched over their fiefdom of the dining room and kitchen, with particular interest in the conduct of the waiters and busboys. At the table was Martin, plus his sister Susan, a woman of about 30, divorced several times, whose relationship to the waiters and busboys was very remote. Then there was Grandma Teitelman, known to all as Grandma, a cranky little old lady, generally unpleasant, who used the same blue hairdresser as Edna. Morris T. came and went quickly and often, supervising the physical operation of the hotel and grounds. Martin, when he wasn't annoying the guests with his jokes, was always there. My new status interfered seriously with ordering extra food, food intended for my busboy and me, and killing livestock would be impossible. Anyone seated at the Family Table had a clear view into my server.

Depending upon the age and socio-economic status of the guests assigned to your station each Sunday evening, you could almost predict the tip you would get for the week. What the guests did not know is that the waiters who returned summer after summer kept track of the tips given to them by specific guests and families who returned summer after summer. This data was shared by the senior waiters who sat with the maître d', the captain and Martin T. late each Sunday afternoon, as they reviewed the check-in slips sent down by Mrs. T. from the front desk. The senior waiters negotiated for certain guests, based upon their tipping history. The fate of each waiter was determined by how each stood with Martin, the captain and the major dean. If they wanted you to make a lot of money, they gave you more people and better tippers. Otherwise you got fewer people and more of those who wore support hosiery.

In addition to any known tipping history of a particular couple, the dining room seat assignment of guests was also influenced by a coding system the front desk used as people checked in. The check-in slips were sent to the dining room and noted several things about each guest in an effort to help the dining room seat people of similar age and socioeconomic status together. It started with which building they were staying in, useful information since the room cost varied widely from building to building. The Main House had the cheapest rooms. Another old white building called Putnam Hall was only slightly more expensive. Bradford Hall was moderately expensive and Washington Hall was for the wealthy. It was air-conditioned. Bradford and Washington Halls had the green hamster tunnels direct to the dining room. The desk clerk (usually Mrs. T.) also factored in her impression of a guest's social station in life, coding it onto the check-in slips. This was sort of a combination of their age, appearance, clothing and whether or not they used a bellhop to assist them or were too cheap and carried their own luggage. Guests were coded with the letters A though D, with plus and minus signs. The A's were younger couples and might not have much money yet. They were generally the ones with young children. B's and B+'s were what a waiter wanted. These were the people in their late 30's to 50's who appeared to have money. Sometimes guests who Mrs. Teitelman would have given a C or C+ based upon advanced age alone would actually get a B- if they appeared wealthy and sophisticated or had rooms in Washington Hall. The C-'s and D's were older and often crotchety. Their tipping habits had not changed since Harry Truman won the White House.

The dining room was a rectangle. When you came in the large doors at the front you were looking the long way down the dining room toward the doors to the kitchen at the back left. The left side of the dining room was mostly wall except for a set of double doors that opened out into the Social Hall and a giant air conditioning unit. Further up along the wall was a small opening giving access to the linen room. Beyond the linen room was a small recess where the coffee machines were and beyond that you cleared the doors into the kitchen. It was the right side of the dining room that was much prettier because it was lined with floor to ceiling windows, sheer curtains and beautiful drapes that were often open. You could look out over the manicured lawns and toward the pool. Clearly guests preferred to sit along the window tables looking out on the lawn as they dined rather than sitting by the front door or near the Social Hall or worse yet up close to the kitchen. So the tables along the window wall or one row in from the windows were where better clientele were always assigned, better according to Mrs. T.'s alphabet and/or their known tipping histories.

The older and less affluent guests were assigned to tables along the inside wall and toward the rear. They had a beautiful view of the kitchen. Close to the kitchen meant closer to death. Those in the middle but toward the rear had a view of the linen room, coffee station, Social Hall or no view at all. Waiters with seniority or influence were assigned the stations whose tables included the windows and "better" tables in the center. Waiters of lower rank, "low scrotum on the totem" as they were known, got the stations along the inside wall and less desirable tables in the center and toward the rear. The captain assigned himself a lot of people, all known good tippers, and worked from the nicest location along the window. He made certain he made a lot of money, even if the hotel was not full that week. As low station waiter, I got the worst tippers, sitting at the least desirable tables. And not very many of them.

But even within the window side of the dining room, there was a bit of a class structure. The serving stations and their tables at the back corner were not favored as much as ones towards the front. Along the windows of the dining room were six distinct waiters' stations, each with its own server. Around each server there would be a cluster of three to six tables, generally seating eight but occasionally seating ten. Only several of those tables would be close to the window, the others would be slightly further into the dining room. It was a long tradition at the Teitelman's Inn to assign one particular station to the captain of the dining room. That server that was second in line along the windows upon entering the dining room. It was always known as the captain's station. Besides having what were anticipated to be the best tippers, the captain would get a full complement of tables, even if the hotel was not full and the other waiters had a reduced number. This way the captain made money no matter what. So being selected as captain of the waiters for the summer meant some serious potential income. My situation now was exactly the opposite.

As a waiter, you did not want unattached people at your tables. All tables seated an even number. Unless there were two assigned to your table, a single person meant an empty seat. You never got a tip from an empty chair. While children ate 60 minutes earlier in a separate dining room with their own waiter, teenagers often wanted to eat with their parents. While it is a truism that most teenagers want nothing to do with their parents and would rather not be seen with them, most are accustomed to eating with them. Better to eat with your parents than a room full of six-year-olds. A waiter, however, did not want teenagers at his table either. The prevailing wisdom was that the tip you got from the parents for serving their teenagers 21 meals was never equal to what you would have gotten if normal humans occupied the same seats. Worse yet, if a couple came with one teenager, one seat at your table would remain empty. But a waiter was more than happy to accept a teenager at his table even if it created an empty seat if she was the same age as the waiter and was gorgeous. An infrequent but not unheard of event, and it was how I met the girl from Rhode Island the previous summer.

As the least senior and thus "low station waiter" my tables were next to the "in" door to the kitchen. I had no teenagers. I had their great-grandparents. The hotel guests assigned to me were all senior, very senior citizens. Many had canes. The first meal I served as a waiter was a disaster. While some of my guests were kind and pleasant, there were others I simply could not please. Nothing I served was right and nothing came fast enough, despite my close proximity to the kitchen. They talked to me while I was trying to remember their orders, wanted numerous substitutions from the written menu and expected me to get it all correct.

On top of my crotchety old guests, I was assigned a busboy with absolutely no prior busboy experience. I had less than two hours to train him. Déjà vu. A nice fellow named David, who came from Israel, he was eager to learn and to help me, but he was no match for the chaos that was our first meal working together. I made so many mistakes on peoples' orders and had trouble getting their substitutions right. We clearly stood out as idiot waiter and busboy. However, it was only the first meal of a 21 meal one-week stay for our guests and only the third week of the summer season. We had time to learn. Many of the other waiters had busboys they were still breaking in.

At about 9:15 p.m., our first meal finally ended. As our guests were leaving after over two hours in the dining room, one big woman probably in her late 70's came toward me. I stopped to find out what she needed. With a very strong European accent she whispered to me that tomorrow morning first thing when she came in for breakfast she wanted me to bring her prunes. I mumbled okay but was too exhausted to really be listening. There was another hour of work ahead of me tonight cleaning up the mess and resetting our tables for the late Tea Room the bellhops would run. Our day would resume tomorrow before 7:00 a.m.

The next morning at 6:40, David and I were back in the dining room setting up for my first breakfast as a waiter. Breakfast had the potential to be an easy meal or a very difficult one. It was the only meal at which guests were not expected to arrive all at the same time. At lunches and dinners a waiter wanted all guests to arrive at once. We liked post time. This way everyone was on the same course. Trips to the kitchen were all appetizers, all soup, all main courses, etc. Guests were actually expected to arrive at lunch and dinner as the dining room opened, and most did. Breakfast was different. Guests had a two-hour window. If your guests arrived for breakfast in a steady stream, the meal would be busy but organized. People around the dining room would be at various stages of their meal so that people waiting for the next items complained less. But if your guests happened to arrive mostly at once, there were too many choices on the breakfast menu to handle without paper and pencil. There were six different juices, various breads for toast, pastries, along with fruits, hot cereals, eggs any way, various omelets, pancakes, etc. Naturally, 20 of our guests arrived within about two minutes of one another. David and I were immediately running after juices, hot cereals, cold cereals, bagels, eggs, omelets, pancakes, toast, French toast, pastries, fresh fruit and coffee.

One of the first guests I approached for her order told me she wanted a six-minute soft-boiled egg. Now I was no chef, but I knew an egg became hard-boiled in about five minutes. So I asked her, "a six-minute soft-boiled egg?" "Yes," she said. She did not find me funny when I asked if she wanted it in cold water for the first four minutes or the last four minutes. Then, one big woman who I did not recognize sat down at one of my tables and motioned me over aggressively. I approached her with a smile and a "Good morning, what can I get for you this morning?" Instantly she exploded with rage, banged her fist on the table hard enough to cause the spoons to become airborne and people around us to look at the commotion. Then she shouted at me in an angry tone "I told you last night I wanted prunes!" I sent David for prunes.

9
BEING A WAITER

Prunes were not something I had spent much of my life thinking seriously about. But the Teitelman's Inn was going to change that. The C- and D guests I served were very fond of prunes. Actually, they were usually pronounced "prumes." So popular were they that a new beverage had been invented to put prume power to work. I believe this beverage to have been invented at this hotel.

Several of my guests began each morning by requesting a small glass of prume juice, a cup of hot water and a tall empty glass. I watched in amazement as they combined the prume juice and hot water into the big glass and drank it down. Evidently hot prune juice has stimulant properties of which I was ignorant and properties that far exceeded plain prume juice or stewed prunes. Since efficient communication between waiter and busboy was critical if service was to be quick, David and I needed a way to communicate to one another that Mrs. So-and-So wanted a small glass of prune juice, a cup of hot water and an empty 12 ounce glass. So I gave this beverage its name. I would now simply tell David to get Mrs. So-and-So a "Royal Flush." The name caught on. I believe that to this day I am famous in Connecticut for having created it.

This concoction was not the only popular item at the hotel. There were others having nothing to do with the fact that Chinese men were cooking kosher Jewish food. For example, a dinner might present pot roast, d.b.a. "braised brisket of beef" as the headliner. Other options included roast chicken, either a "roast top" or a "roast bottom," boiled chicken, either a "boiled top" or a "boiled bottom." Other nights had steak or roast beef as the headliner. But an item that was on the menu every night made me hold my breath when I served it so as to avoid gagging. No, it wasn't meat loaf. It was boiled beef. Boiled beef or beef flanken, known affectionately to its friends as just "Flanken", was for me an Olympic level competitor to meatloaf as to which made me most likely to gag.

Flanken, often pronounced as "flonkin," was not the color I had always assumed that beef was supposed to be. Flanken was gray. It included the bone. It looked sick, like the cow had died of cancer before it got to the slaughterhouse. It reminded me of the old joke about why Jews don't eat cured ham. "No one tells you what it was sick with before it was cured." Flanken was served with boiled potatoes and I had to remember not to reach for it until the chef had sprinkled on the parsley. But in an odd way, people ordering items like boiled bottoms or flanken made the waiter's job easier. Waiters were required to keep the guests' orders in their heads. We were prohibited from writing our orders down.

Having waiters remember the orders was part of the hotel's idea of classy service. It had very much the opposite effect the hotel hoped for.

The general rule was to take orders from one table at a time and rush to the kitchen and get in line. But waiters want to maximize the efficiency of each trip to the kitchen. Since the chef would let you out with 12 main dishes, three tables of eight guests each could be done as two trips of 12 orders. So while it was frowned upon by Martin T., some waiters took orders from a table and a half at the same time. I wasn't that experienced yet and being right next to the kitchen did have one obvious advantage. For me, taking orders from eight people without paper and pencil seemed like enough.

A really good waiter would not only return with the correct items cooked as requested, but would recall who got what as well as any requested substitutions. I found that taking orders from eight people at one table without paper was very easy, unless you wanted to get their orders right. In my early days as a waiter I was content just to return with the correct items and ask "Who gets well done roast beef?" That's where the flanken and boiled bottoms came in handy. The physical appearance and personality of some of my guests seem to correlate well with their choice of foods. In plain English, some people just reminded me of flanken or boiled bottoms. That made these items easier to remember when I was on line in the kitchen. When back in the dining room, I seemed to know which individuals the items belonged to, just by looking at them. Actually the trick we used to remember our orders was to remember how many people you have taken orders from, rely on the fact that some orders (and people) stood out in your memory, and then subtract to get the number of normal items. Doing this technically reduced the actual number of items you had to recall. This method worked extremely well when brisket was the headliner, since it only came one way. Twelve people, two boiled bottoms, a roast top, a roast bottom and a flanken, left seven who must be getting brisket. The system broke down a bit however, when steak or roast beef was the headliner. The rares, medium rares, mediums, medium wells, wells or end cuts did not integrate nicely into this approach. Unlike with brisket, there were too many alternative ways of wanting steak or roast beef cooked. Often I just ordered a lot of mediums, since there was natural variation among them anyway and there was always the trick I had learned to change their appearance by drying and flipping them.

No memory system worked well when people wanted to substitute a different vegetable for the one that came standard with the entrée they ordered. I might remember the odd vegetable, but it was hard to remember which entrée it went with or who was getting it. This I assumed was the reason the hotel wanted college kids as waiters, our high IQs. I cheated by bringing the odd vegetable, if I remembered it, in a separate dish and then asking "Who gets the ...?" In addition to the ladies who wanted a third piece of cake, but saccharin for their coffee, the folks that wanted the meat very, very rare stood out. One guest wanted his steak the way I thought only the French ate meat, purple but warm. I wondered if CPR could have revived it. Another guest whose order always stood out was the man who ate two raw eggs each morning, before he ate cooked eggs for breakfast. He poked a hole with a fork and sucked out the contents. Every morning! He died (the following year) from his first heart attack, fortunately not in the dining room.

I made a lot of mistakes and ran a lot of exchanges to the kitchen, making what was intended to be fancy service into what is often described in Yiddish as "schlock" (cheap, trashy or of low quality) service. At some meals the dining room might as well have had sawdust or peanut shells on the floor; we weren't any classier. Some waiters even gave up taking orders altogether and simply speculated on what their guests might want. One waiter, Joe Goldman, could carry five or six main dishes full of food up his left arm without letting the food from one dish contact the bottom of any other dish. He could get into the kitchen first by not wasting time taking orders from anyone. He would simply speculate and order one or two extras. The kitchen had no system for comparing the number of guests he was serving against the number of entrées he ordered. What he did not use got buried in his bus box or hid so he could eat it later. He'd then use the dry and flip method to make meat appear more well done or send his busboy for exchanges when his bad guesses could not be corrected with his side towel. This worked pretty well for Joe. His judgment of what his people were going to eat in relation to what they looked like, combined with their temptation to accept whatever they saw him carrying as he circled their table, let him please them. He probably made only a few more exchanges than the rest of us but most of his guests got served fast and therefore tipped well. I concentrated more on remembering my orders and zeroing in on who looked like a boiled beef flanken or a boiled bottom. Anyway, Joe's method of serving was illegal, so I avoided using it unless I had forgotten all of my orders.

Every so often I found myself on line in the kitchen with eight different orders stored too loosely in my brain. Three meatloaf, one no gravy, two roast top, one roast bottom, one boiled top and one boiled bottom. Hold the carrots on the boiled bottom. Then disaster struck. Another waiter on line told a joke or a waiter fell and dropped a tray full of food. When I was done laughing, I had absolutely no idea what my dinner orders were. This would also happen if I stopped silently rehearsing my orders for a moment and paid too much attention to a waiter in front of me on line as he ordered. Especially if the kitchen was noisy and he shouted his orders to the chef, his orders and mine would sort of merge in my head. I could also lose my orders if I clowned around. In the morning, guests could have any style omelet they wished, including but not limited to smoked salmon, onion, mushroom, cheese, tomato, loose, dry, or any combination of the above. So one morning just for fun, I spewed out my long and fragile list of breakfast orders to the chef and included a watermelon omelet in the list between the lox and onion and the cheese. The chef stopped dead in his tracks and looked at me. He had now forgotten my orders. So had I. Many of the boys behind me were so busy laughing, they forgot theirs as well. I got screamed at by the breakfast chef.

I could also lose my orders by simply trusting the chef. Almost always, he got the orders correct. So once I dumped my orders to him after rehearsing them for the last ten minutes, I would forget them. But once in a while the chef got mixed up. He would then ask me to repeat the orders. I would stand there like an idiot not remembering. The only solution then was to speculate.

To help me remember the food orders, I needed to teach the people I was serving to order correctly, that is, order in the manner I wanted them to. This was probably an early sign of things to come for me, now a behavioral psychologist. Because I had their orders circling precariously in my head, the guests had to learn how to cooperate with me as I received additional orders. All questions about the food or how it was prepared had to be asked before any ordering actually began. No kibitzing. Guests were to make up their minds quickly, so that I could avoid being the last one on line in the kitchen and getting hung. Guests were not to speak to one another while I was taking their orders and other than announcing their order, they were not to speak to me. Whatever direction we started in, we had to continue in that direction around the table. No ordering out of turn. No "my wife will have." Everyone gave their own order. They were not to request substitutions. If Brussels sprouts came with your dinner, you did not ask to have carrots and peas instead. Whether they were available or not was irrelevant, it mixed me up. No changing your mind once you gave me your order, even if I was still at your table. I tallied in my head as I went around the table. Addition, no subtraction. A violation of any one of these rules could cause me to forget all of the orders and have to start over again going around the table. If I forgot the orders, I did not want to take the time to go around the table again. It could make me look incompetent to my guests and nobody wanted to be last waiter on line in the kitchen. I would sometimes decide, oh, fuck it, and speculate instead. Dangerous, but less time-consuming.

When attempting to teach guests to order properly, I

found that Mrs. T.'s coding system predicted the outcome. Later in my career as a waiter I learned that teaching the B+ guests to order by my rules was easiest. At the beginning of the week, I would kind of hint at what I needed them to do and hope they would comply. Guests who had been at the hotel before often remembered how difficult this was for the waiter and would encourage other guests to behave. Psychologists call it peer pressure.

When training my guests to order, if anyone broke a rule, I might make believe I forgot all of the orders, even if I had not, and start taking the orders from the entire table all over again. Using this as a punishment procedure wasted time and was costly to me and to them at that meal, but, doing it once or twice at the beginning of their week at the hotel caused most guests to learn and the rest of the week went smoothly. But my first summer, the summer of the C- and D crowd, was hard. These folks took longer to make up their minds and more often had questions and substitutions. But they caught on by the end of the week. Once I had my guests ordering properly, I could kibitz with them a little and still keep the orders straight in my head. When they asked if the flanken was good tonight, I always said no. If they asked how the liver was tonight, I promised I'd never give them a "bum steer." When Lenny, who owned a gas station in Stanbury, was about to give me his order, I asked if he wanted regular or high test. The goal was always the same. Make them like you in order to increase your tips, but train them to make your job easier. I accomplished little, however, with the guests who ordered nearly every item on the extensive menu. They would eat a bite or two, push the plate aside, and then try the next dish.

Most waiters had a favorite tray they used. While all of the trays looked the same, kind of a very large oval pizza pan, aluminum or galvanized steel with a heavy lip around the edge, some seemed better balanced than others. Older ones might buckle up and down in the center when carried heavily loaded with food. That was dangerous and even more so if the waiter was drunk. Waiters typically marked their favorite tray, not by urinating on it but by scratching something cryptic on the bottom. Before each meal, the waiter would search through the pile of washed trays in the back of the kitchen and find his. The best tray I found at the hotel had "fram" scratched on the underside. I always tried to use that tray. Like everything else at the hotel, once you had what you needed, you hid it. Waiters and busboys would fight over trays so once again I found great value in the use of my Buick's large trunk.

The combination of kosher hotel and Chinese chefs produced some interesting results. Both cultures have a food that is basically ground beef inside a closed noodle. In one culture they are called Won Tons, in the other they are Kreplach. To a waiter or busboy who didn't really care, they looked the same. To Shing Chen, still the number one chef, they were very different. If you told him you needed an order of Won Tons when he thought he made Kreplach, or vice-versa, he became so offended that if you didn't lose part of your hand to a meat cleaver, you certainly blew any chance of getting guest food for yourself for quite some time. You were then on Shing Chen's list, the one he called a "Shit-a-Waita."

If there was ever a cross between the two cultures that worked very well, it was the kosher egg roll. Made with chicken instead of pork, they were delicious. Usually served in the Social Hall when there was a fancy large buffet lunch in place of the sit down lunch in the dining room, waiters would jockey for the opportunity to carry them out from the kitchen and supervise their short life in a stainless steel pan above a Sterno. Bringing them from the kitchen, through the dining room and to the adjacent Social Hall provided a waiter with a relatively easy opportunity to eat a half dozen or so along the way. They were small. They could almost be swallowed whole. No chewing. So coveted were these kosher egg rolls that hotel guests would line up at the serving table before the food was even brought out, hoping to get a few before they were gone.

Although Shing Chen made plenty of egg rolls, there were never enough to satisfy everyone. Something about the kosher Chinese food brought out the oriental behavior in our guests; once the egg rolls were brought out, there was no longer any such thing as a line. Particularly the prune juice and support hosiery crowd would push and shove trying to get a few of these delicacies. The interactions often got nasty and according to the New York Times, Yiddish is second only to Hungarian for its very graphic swears and curses. But only once did I see the ultimate; a pushing fight between a little old man and a big old lady, as they neared the finish line for the remaining egg rolls. The man got knocked to the floor.

Not all of the guests at the hotel were Jewish, of course. Many Non-Jews frequented the place as well. A student of human social behavior and cultural diversity even early in my career, I noticed that you could distinguish the Jews from the Non-Jews by their behavior each time we had a buffet. It was simple. The Jews were crowded around the food tables, pushing and shoving. The Non-Jews were crowded around the bar, no pushing. Herein lies the great social significance of Shing Chen's kosher egg rolls. They were the great equalizer. Everybody pushed for them.

10
THE CHILDREN'S WAITER

If the hotel had 350 guests for the week, there might be 15-30 children among them. While the hotel wasn't the best place I could think of for a family vacation, it did have a day camp, a few counselors and a kiddie pool. The children ate in a separate dining room that adjoined the main dining room and had their own waiter and busboy. They ate one hour before the main dining room opened. No one wanted to be the children's waiter. First, it had no social status. As a teenage male, being assigned to feed children did not impress your peers. Second, Martin was known to use assignment as children's waiter for a week as punishment for things like killing livestock or getting caught chewing. It could even be more effective than making us scrub the dining room.

The typical tip a waiter received for serving an adult couple for a week in the dining room ranged from $10 to $14, if his guests were born post World War I. That's two people for 21 meals each for 24 to 33 cents per person per meal, and considered a reasonable tip! If you had three full tables, or twelve couples, a waiter could expect to make from $120 to $168 that week. His busboy, about $80 to $120. If the hotel was busy and the waiter well-liked by the bosses, he might have four tables of eight, an estimated $160 to $224 for the week. His busboy might see $7 to $10 per couple from the post WW1 crowd or between $112 and $160 per week at best. Good money for a teenager in the late 1960's.

If you had the B or B+ guests, each might tip the waiter $16-30 per couple per week, although $20 was most common. That was a lot of money. And more than once later in my career at the hotel I had a couple give me a $50 bill for the week. One man was known to all the waiters to tip $50 for him and his wife for the week, but gave it to you differently. On Sunday evening when he arrived, he tore a $50 bill in half in front of you and handed you one half. He then told you that if the service was good, you would get the other half next Sunday. Can you imagine doing that in a restaurant today? The C's and C-'s were often under $10 per couple for the waiter and still less for the poor busboy.

While the typical waiter serving reasonable guests anticipated $10 to $14 per couple per week, if they had 2 teenagers with them in the main dining room he almost never got an additional $10.   He generally received just an extra $3 or $4 each. If there was only one teenager, the waiter then had an empty seat at the table. Clearly, teenagers were worth less than adults. (And that is still true in so many ways.)

Tips to the waiter for serving the little monsters in the children's dining room were generally even worse. Three or four dollars per week per kid was typical – for serving them 21 meals. The children's waiter would make less than the majority of busboys in the main dining room and had all of the problems that go along with feeding children. To make matters worse, they could order almost any item that the adults could order. Though the children's waiter had more time off, he made a lot less money and still had to do Gigolo Duty.

When Martin did not assign the job of children's waiter as punishment, he sought a volunteer. The only way he got one was to allow you to be children's waiter and adult waiter. He'd have a busboy do all the cleanup after you served the children. Then you ran into the main dining room to serve the adults. Your busboy had to do all of your setup work in the main dining room. If you took both jobs you got virtually no time off between meals at all and worked 7 days per week from 6:30 a.m. until 9:30 p.m. But you could make a lot of money. The parents also tipped better for their kids if you were also their own waiter. I occasionally volunteered to work both jobs. The trick was how to manage your "guests," ranging from toddlers to almost teenagers.

First, you had to get their attention. Then, do not tell them they could have anything they wanted. That would be chaos. I'd announce "We have corn flakes, scrambled eggs and pancakes today." "Who wants cornflakes? Raise your hand." "Who wants pancakes? Raise your hand." Everyone was given an orange juice. That worked well, except for the occasional kid who actually thought he was at a hotel and wanted a different cereal or different juice or had learned there was more than one way an egg could be prepared. I would discuss it with him/her privately and say ok, but you will have to wait. He/she would intentionally be served last. I had two objectives. One was to teach him not to do that again. The other was to get all of the other kids eating from the limited list I offered before they saw anyone with something different. This way I minimized the chances of a revolt against the limited choices I had offered. I had to be particularly careful doing this with the older children, as they tended to speak up. I often took them into my confidence and explained what I was trying to do. I'd ask if they minded waiting until last so as to help me avoid chaos with younger ones. Since most of the older kids disliked the younger ones anyway, especially their siblings, they were generally cooperative. Other than long hours, I liked the challenge of being children's waiter and I loved the extra money.

11
JOB SECURITY

Martin Teitelman was our boss, but he was not someone you could easily like. His laugh had tonal characteristics that I had never heard before. It was a deep, loud, throated noise, usually repeated three to five times, with audible intakes of air between each. Actually it was not unlike sounds later described in a book by Jane Goodall. She called them "pant-hoots." He could easily be heard over the roar of hundreds of people eating and socializing in the dining room. When Martin sat down with a table of the hotel's guests and told them a joke, I was convinced it was his own laugh following the joke that the guests were laughing at, and not the joke itself. I managed to get along with Martin. I'm not entirely sure why, but there were at least two contributing factors.

During my second summer at the hotel, my first summer as a waiter, Martin purchased a gazebo for his backyard. He had a brick ranch-style home built the year before. Located about six miles from the hotel, his house was beautiful. I had been to the house once or twice when sent on an errand to pick up or deliver something. We all knew he had purchased an elaborate gazebo, because he could be easily overheard telling hotel guests about it, whether they were interested or not. It seemed, however, that this eight-sided, screened-in polygon was too complicated for Martin to assemble. Issues of symmetry, a latching door, the weather-tight roof and the stakes to keep it earth-bound required a level of mechanical skill believed to be carried on the same gene that endows one with a normal laugh. Martin was missing that gene. While not mechanically inclined, he was more mechanically reclined since he liked to sit and watch other people do the work. Martin was capable, however, of deducing that anyone who could replace a fender on a Volkswagen could probably assemble a gazebo. I was offered no choice.

One sunny afternoon I was assigned to appear at Martin's home and help him assemble the gazebo. Of course it was on my own time, my precious few hours off between lunch and supper and without compensation. Normally at that time of day, if I was able to escape the dining room, I would either be sleeping, swimming or pursuing some member of the female persuasion. As Martin liked to say, however, "Lincoln freed the slaves in the South; this is Connecticut." I only had difficulty with two aspects of the assembly. One was in following the written gazebo assembly instructions and the other was with Martin's efforts to help. Once I abandoned the directions and got Martin to step back, it went well. In just an hour and a half, it was up and looking good. Martin was impressed with my skill at assembling the gazebo, particularly the fact that I had used almost all of the parts. Fortunately for me, I suppose, was that it soon occurred to Martin that he would need me to disassemble the thing after Labor Day and reassemble it next summer. I now had the beginnings of job security.

My third summer at Teitelman's Inn, my second summer as a waiter, a lot of things changed. When I returned to the hotel in mid-June, I learned that a number of the older waiters would not be returning. Many had graduated college and went on to better things. We learned that Michael Sheffield had been drafted out of law school, despite his best efforts to gain admission to Rabbinical School and/or have a Boston surgeon remove one kidney to ensure a continued deferment. He was in Vietnam. I had moved up in the ranks and so was assigned a station along the windows, though toward the back. I was doing okay making money, although still nothing like the waiters further toward the front. Only a few of my guests ate prunes.

I had worked a number of the holiday weekends during the off-season, when the hotel was desperate for experienced staff. Martin would guarantee me a certain amount of money to encourage me to come up from New York. Still driving my '55 Buick and still at NYU, I needed the money. Typically, he promised $125 for a three-day weekend; if I did not make it in tips, he would make up the difference. Seeing me during the year when they needed me and seeing me for my third summer, had the Teitelmans liking me a little, at least as much as they seemed to like any of the hired help.

With the Buick stripped of most chrome and repainted in flat, dark grey primer, weekend trips to the hotel occasionally got me an opportunity to interact with the police. One state trooper pulled me over for a spot check. When I asked why he singled me out, he replied that "My car looked like a shitbox." There's that word again! I challenged him to look under my car and see its solid mechanical condition or check out all of the money I had obviously invested in the interior. Did he think I would do that with a mechanically unsafe car? He backed off after checking my license and registration.

A situation that worried me more occurred months later when the Westchester Parkway Police pulled me over on my way to Connecticut. Initially, two officers got out of their grey and white. One was quite young and the other older, heavier, with grey hair and lots of stripes, tassels and emblems on his uniform and what looked like pancakes on his shoulders. I knew that two of my tires no longer met the legal standard for the amount of remaining tread. Simply put, a couple of them were almost bald. Perhaps I had a chance of talking my way out of a ticket with the younger officer, but if he was in training or under the supervision of the older, decorated one, I figured I was cooked. But only the younger one approached me. The older one got back in the car. Again, I was told this was a spot check. He examined my documents and walked slowly around the car. My license and registration were fine, but my tires were not. Ticket time, unless I could talk my way out.

I explained to the officer that I was aware of the condition of the tires. I was heading for Connecticut to work as a waiter that weekend, knowing I would make enough money to buy new tires. I pointed out to him that if he gave me a ticket, the money I earned would have to go toward the ticket, instead of new tires. I challenged him as to which was more important to him, giving me a ticket or having me be safe. He looked at me, a bit shocked. I assured him that if he let me go without the ticket, he could pull me over next time he spotted me and I'd be proud to show him my new tires. I told him what days and times I traveled the same route on my way to and from NYU. He could spot check me again. I emphasized that it was his decision; issuing a ticket or my safety. He actually let me go, warning me he'd be watching for me. I thanked him and encouraged him to watch for me. I headed for Connecticut. With money I borrowed on Friday night in anticipation of tips on Sunday, I did get new tires in Tom's Ferry on Saturday at a company that sold retreads. For $40 total, I got four brand new retreaded tires. They looked great with big white walls. Only one problem. There was a tendency for the new treads to separate from the tire. In other words, the new rubber might peel off the tire. But the company was nice about it. They'd replace a tire that came apart. I just hoped the tires didn't come apart while I was doing 60.

Some of the weekends at the hotel during off-season had me working weddings. That was a different kind of an event. In some ways it was easier on the waiters in that the menu was limited. Generally, the wedding guests had only two entrée choices and there were no alternative vegetables to substitute. Science had not yet discovered gluten allergies and so we had no real need to accommodate anyone. Just saccharin instead of sugar. When I worked a wedding, management seemed to always pick me to lace the head table. We just pushed a bunch of rectangular wooden tables end to end and put lots of tablecloths on them sideways, so the fronts reached the floor. Then someone unrolled miles of white lace while I crawled on my knees along the front of the tables with a stapler and attached the lace to the table's top edge. It actually looked nice when it was done.

It only got really chaotic when we were doing two weddings on the same day. It meant breaking everything down after the first wedding and then setting up the next one. All of the lace had to be done over again, since the tablecloths usually had food stains from wedding number one. If people were having a good time at wedding one, it was hard to get them to leave so that we could set up for wedding two. Martin had the solution. The hotel used one giant air conditioning unit to cool both the dining room and the adjoining Social Hall. The giant AC unit stood on the floor against the wall between the dining room and the Social Hall, looking like Gort in the 1951 movie "The Day The Earth Stood Still," starring Michael Rennie as Klaatu. It was used to cool both rooms, but only one at a time. While it cooled one room, it expelled the heat into the other. The Social Hall was used as the wedding chapel and the reception was in the dining room. Martin's method of getting a wedding party to break up after the meal was to reverse Gort so that it now heated the room the wedding party was in.

The best part of the weddings I worked was when all of the waiters came out from the kitchen in a conga line, each carrying a tray with 34 cups of flaming cherries jubilee. The lights would be turned down and it looked spectacular, except when a waiter caught his sleeve on fire and came out flaming along with the cherries. I told the bride and groom that they could always remember that their wedding had flaming waiters. Flaming had a different meaning in those days.

One of the other more memorable weekends I worked was the bachelor party Martin threw for Marek Zaslavski, owner of the Stanbury Bakery. The party was for Marek's second wedding. It included a live performance by members of the 40's vocal group, the Inkspots. Some people said having the Inkspots there was a big deal. To quote from one of their songs, "… I didn't care." The party also had a steak dinner, a stripper, hookers brought in from East Hartford, Connecticut using Washington Hall (the high-priced guest rooms) and a group package Martin negotiated with the hookers for all interested waiters and busboys. Martin made a point of inviting Jim Ogorek, the local constable. I was never exactly clear what a constable was, since we didn't have any in the Bronx. When Jim visited the hotel to see Martin, he would stand in front of the waiters and busboys and challenge us to punch him in the stomach. It was amazing. Jim was huge and his abdomen was impenetrable. He never flinched. The hotel often invited Constable Ogorek to private parties during the off-season, to reduce the chances of a police raid during these events. Having the local constable invited was assumed to keep the real cops quiet.

As much as being there for the Teitelmans during occasional weekends in the off-season and being in charge of Martin's gazebo gave me job security, toward the end of July of my second summer as a waiter, something happened that changed everything. Martin approached me in confidence one day. He appeared pale and very nervous; scared actually. He confided that he was in the hole to his bookie for over $14,000 and the bookie had some friends with short necks in the money collection business. He was forced to find a quick way of coming up with the money. His parents did not know and he intended to keep it that way. Since a loan shark would only get him in deeper, he needed cheap money. He found a way to get two banks in Tom's Ferry, Connecticut to give him the loan he wanted, interest-free. The banks, however, had no idea that they were lending Martin money, at least not for a while.

Martin explained that he had opened a personal checking account at the Tom's Ferry branch of the Connecticut Bank and Trust, (CB&T). Across the street at another bank, the Tom's Ferry Bank & Trust (TFB&T), he also opened a personal checking account. He then wrote a check for $14,000 on his CB&T account and cashed it at the TFB&T. The Tom's Ferry Bank & Trust cashed the check without question based on the fact the manager knew Morris and Edna Teitelman and that the hotel had accounts with both banks and a good credit history. To cover the CB&T check, he deposited a check for $14,000 at CB&T written on his TFB&T account. In this way, he extracted $14,000 cash from the banking system and paid the bookie. Martin figured that all he had to do to maintain this interest-free loan was to make a deposit every day in each bank with a check for $14,000 drawn on the bank across the street.

This was where Martin found a second use for me and why he first confided in me about his bookie problem. Martin feared that after a time, the tellers in these small town banks would notice something odd about his deposits, both their regularity and the constant amount. He wanted to change that, hoping he could avoid suspicion and keep them from bringing the matter to their respective manager's attention. So Martin decided to solicit my assistance. He wanted me to do some of his banking.

The town of Tom's Ferry was 12 miles from the hotel and my break between breakfast and lunch was often not longer than 40 minutes. In exchange for doing his banking and to give me the time to do it, Martin assigned other busboys to help my busboy do some of my breakfast clean-up and lunch setup work. While this caused my status with Martin to rise, it caused my friendship with a number of busboys to suffer. They were angry at being assigned to help my busboy do my work. I was not the captain. They had no explanation beyond that I was running errands for Martin. But every other day? In an expanding effort to keep either bank from noticing what he was up to, Martin began to vary the size of each deposit, so that it was $14,000 plus or minus $200 or $300 cash. Sometimes he would break the big deposit into several smaller checks, but always drawn on the bank across the street.

My job when he sent me to the banks was to try to use a different teller at each bank than he had used the day before. Martin would describe the teller he used yesterday and I would describe the teller I used today. Normally, one gets on the shortest line at the bank, not the line of a particular teller. It looks odd when you purposely get on the longer line in a small bank. While insane, the system seemed to work. Martin had extracted a lot of money from the banks without an official loan and the money was interest free. The bookie was happy and Martin remained alive and with functional knees. Now I understood why Martin was always in the corner of the dining room in the booth and on the pay phone. He didn't dare use the hotel phone in the dining room, as his mother often manned the switchboard. She had to place all calls off grounds and could of course listen in.

The banking scheme that Martin sucked me into worked fine for about two weeks. I was not happy doing this. I'd rather have been assembling gazebos. Then one day in early August, Martin took me aside just before supper. Again he was very upset and frightened. It seemed that the CB&T manager had phoned the Tom's Ferry Bank & Trust manager to discuss Martin Teitelman's checks. When they realized the scam, the CB&T manager phoned Martin to inform him that if he did not appear at one of the two banks with $14,000 in cash before 3:00 p.m. the following day, he would be going to jail.

Evidently his technique for extracting money from the banks was illegal. Martin could not come up with that much money. Circumstances now forced Martin to develop another scheme, and this one too, had a role for me. I, of course, was now wondering if I'd be indicted along with Martin for his first scheme, or just be identified as an unindicted co-conspirator. I really didn't want to hear about the latest one.

July had gone by and the hotel had been busy. While poor at gambling and poor at gazebos, Martin was okay at math. He had done some figuring and estimated how much money he could assemble if he could just borrow all of the money the waiters and busboys working for him had already made that summer. He just needed a front man to borrow it from them, someone they trusted enough to lend money to and who would say it was for himself. No one was to know the money was for Martin. He imagined me to be that front man. He also wanted to borrow everything I had already made this summer. Then, he wanted a commitment from me that I would turn over to him most of what I made during each of the upcoming weeks for the rest of the summer, as well as any additional money I could borrow from the other boys as August progressed. He even offered suggestions as to what I could say to the other waiters as an explanation. He promised to return all of the money, mine and the money I borrowed for him from the other boys, at the end of the Labor Day weekend.

In no uncertain terms, I told Martin to perform an impossible sex act on himself. There was no way in hell I would borrow money from the other waiters and busboys with some cock and bull story of why I needed it and then give Martin the money. I did not trust Martin that much. Nor was I or any of the other waiters working at the hotel just for fun. We were working hard to earn money towards our college tuition. I was contributing about 40% of what my parents were paying for my tuition at NYU and was financing the bottomless pit known as my '55 Buick. To risk my money alone was madness, never mind the debt I would have to the other waiters and busboys. What if Martin did not repay me at the end of the summer? What if he gambled away even more money? What if he died, with or without the help of the bookie? The dilemma I faced, however, was that I could not entirely say no to Martin and get away with it. He wouldn't fire me, but I knew that he would see to it I made very little money from this point on if I refused to help him. I'd have fewer guests assigned to my station each week and I'd be serving more prumes. Plus he did not leave me alone. He kept asking, and then pleading. He was genuinely convinced he was going to prison.

As it was my second summer as a waiter, I was not yet making a king's ransom. Clearly, if Martin was waiting for my money every Sunday, he would see to it that I had a lot available. I agreed to go along with his request, but only on my terms. I expressed to him my concern that if I went along with this and then he was killed driving drunk on Route 305 one night, or by a subcontractor to his bookie, I needed proof to provide Martin's wife and Morris and Edna Teitelman that Martin owed me many thousands of dollars. I envisioned myself laughed at, a kid approaching these people in their 60's with a story about how their dead thirty-five-year-old son had borrowed $7,000 from me and other boys through me. Anybody tough enough to make their insurance agent share his commission was probably not easy to do business with. I knew I needed a contract. Martin agreed and I drew one up. It was the first contract I had ever tried to write, but I felt confident about what it had to say. It had to be detailed. It must specify the amount he was borrowing, that it was cash, who he was borrowing it from, when he had borrowed it and what the source of the money was. It further described that the contract would be amended each Sunday if additional funds were borrowed and that full repayment was required by 3 p.m. this coming Labor Day. I never thought to include a penalty for default. I wanted it witnessed, but that created a problem for Martin. He did not want anyone else to know.

Other than a witness to the contract, Martin agreed to all of my terms without a complaint. I did not dare imagine him actually defaulting. Then I hit him with two other conditions. I was going to promise each waiter and busboy who lent me money, interest equal to what we were earning in the Farmers National Bank in Stanbury, where many of us kept our savings all summer. Although one month at 3% annual interest was not serious money, for me it was a matter of principle. Again Martin agreed. All of this was in the contract I wrote out by hand and Martin willingly signed and dated. Then I laid out the final condition, the only one that was not in writing. I was done eating the shit staff food. From this day forth, I would have the right to eat guest food providing I did not flaunt it. I would not, however, eat in the back of the kitchen near the pot washers and I was to be granted the right to chew. I wanted to be promoted to a human being. Martin agreed, this time reluctantly.

Purposely, I was only slightly successful borrowing from the other waiters. I did not ask for as much as Martin wanted and did not ask very many of them. I told Martin that it was all they agreed to lend me. I didn't like the liability. I don't recall exactly how much I borrowed from them in total but I do recall using a story about needing to pay my NYU tuition early, before my scholarship money came in and that my parents did not have the money at this time. My scholarship money was due in a few weeks and I could pay them back, by Labor Day at the latest. And I would pay interest. I drew up a contract with each of the boys I borrowed from. Not all of the boys I asked agreed to lend me money, but most did. The next day, after breakfast, we all went to the bank in

Stanbury and made cash withdrawals. I took only some of what I had saved, combined it with their money, and gave it to Martin. A few trusted me enough to say the contract was unnecessary, but I insisted on creating one. Martin and I added the detailed amounts to the contract.

For the remaining weeks of the summer Martin saw to it that guests assigned to me were known good tippers, much more so than would have ever been the case. I don't know how he explained to the maître d' and captain why he was doing it. I suspected that perhaps they were involved in his scheme in some way as well since the amount I provided did not meet all of Martin's need. Then, every Sunday afternoon as this week's guests said goodbye and gave us our tips, Martin pursued me to find out how much money I had made. He was asking before I even counted it. For two reasons, I never gave him the true numbers. First, I wanted to limit how much of my money he had. Second, I knew he would see to it that I made even more next week. I refused to ask any of my friends for more and gave Martin the most plausible reason I could come up with for why. I explained to Martin that asking them for more money would be inconsistent with the story I had given them in the first place.

I sweated over this arrangement for weeks, imagining the unimaginable. What would happen if, at the end of the summer, Martin did not have the money or only had part of the money? What if he denied the entire arrangement? Did I make the greatest mistake of my life? But Labor Day came around and Martin returned my money, plus all of the money I had borrowed on his behalf and the interest I had insisted on. All cash. I was very relieved. I never asked him where he got the money to repay me or how he squared things at the banks. I did not care. I had made a small fortune as a waiter that summer with Martin looking out for himself, through me. All I had to do now before returning to New York was disassemble his gazebo. When I reflected on what had happened, I realized how well this hotel was preparing me for adult life.

12
LIVING WELL

When I arrived at the hotel that summer, weeks prior to Martin's money issue, I had purposely arrived early enough to look for a nice place to live. Representing myself and four other waiters, I began calling real estate agents in the Kirby area to see about renting a cottage around one of the lakes. An agent named John Breslow was decent with me, and showed me a two-bedroom cottage right on Lake Gilmer.

The hotel was at the western end of the lake and the cottage was at the eastern end. Getting there was a slow, circuitous trip of about four miles. But the cottage was lovely. Painted yellow, it was located on a corner lot. It had a small shed/boat house behind it for storing fishing or boat stuff and it had 40 feet of its own private beach. Since it was on ground a bit higher than the water, it was built into the hill. Accessed from the back of the kitchen was a porch running the length of the house, overlooking the water and providing a beautiful view. The place had a telephone; we simply had to take responsibility for it and agree to pay the bills. Gas cooking was included. The cottage was fully furnished, including a refrigerator, beds and a sofa that opened into an extra bed in the dinette.

With little negotiating needed on my part, Mr. Breslow agreed to rent it to me on behalf of the five of us for $400 for the 10-week summer season. I signed the lease. That he agreed so readily to rent the place to five teenage boys surprised me. I wondered if I looked that responsible or if the owner was desperate. Perhaps someone was hoping we burned it down so they could collect the insurance. In hindsight, it was ten years before the Animal House movie came out, so maybe the owner was just naïve. With some quick math, I calculated that this gorgeous place divided by ten weeks and five boys would cost us each only $8 per week. What a deal and he only wanted a $50 security deposit. The previous year I had lived in a rooming house in Stanbury. That worked out well except that every single time the woman who owned the house saw me, she greeted me with "Remember, no girls allowed in your room." No such restrictions here. Compared to the Staff House or the room in Stanbury, this was heaven.

Previous summers I sometimes slept elsewhere, since my aunt and uncle were less than thirty minutes away. I really liked my cousins and my aunt and uncle were always very nice to me. They had a finished room in their basement that had an outside entrance. My grandfather was a skilled carpenter and he had helped them remodel the basement. My aunt gave me a key so that I could come and go at all hours without disturbing them. Often, I fled the Staff House my first summer or my rented room the second summer and stayed in my aunt and uncle's basement for the night. There was a half bath off the kitchen and of course there was food in the refrigerator. The drive from my aunt's back to the hotel at 6:00 a.m. often took me through some of the worst fog I had ever seen. I never recall it being foggy in the Bronx, but in this part of Connecticut at 6:00 a.m. in the summer, the driving could be so bad that you had to keep the car door open, look at the ground and follow the yellow lines. Having a cottage on a lake this summer and so close to the hotel was a thrill.

This lovely cottage I rented from John Breslow was not without logistical problems, however. There were two double beds and a single bed for five guys. We also needed a system to inform one another when one of us had company for the evening. None of this was a serious problem as we were so busy, so tired and usually so drunk that very little mattered. Occasionally my roommate, a good guy just over five feet tall named Louie Sternberg, was actually in our bed. Louie was another influential individual at the hotel; Al Sternberg, our salad man, famous for his coleslaw, was his uncle. Whenever we partied or were invited to a party at a cottage that other waiters had rented on another lake, Louie got us the J&B. He might have been short, but he had turned 21 and had an ID to prove it. Often when Louie was drunk, he could be found standing on top of a table, singing as loud as he could, accompanying the record by the Kingsmen, "Louie Louie." Our Louie sang what he insisted were the correct words.

The trip back and forth on the curvy road around the lake to our cottage before and after each meal and at least once more each night required cautious driving. But I could relax once I got there. My belongings were safe. I trusted the guys I shared the house with and we could lock our door. Best of all was the back porch. I would come back to the cottage after lunch each day, sit in a rocking chair on the porch and look out over the lake. It was so peaceful. I would eat a bowl of dry cereal while rocking. We had a lot of dry cereal at the cottage. We also had a lot of cantaloupe, a lot of clean sheets, towels, soap, toilet paper, silverware, dishes, crackers, pillows and five row boats, all "borrowed" from the hotel. It seemed that having a cottage changed our needs. "Borrowing" from the hotel was no longer simply a survival tactic, it was now an industry. We needed a lot of things to keep our cottage well stocked and running smoothly.

Liberating the expanded list of necessary items from the hotel offered new challenges. When it was my turn to obtain a bag of clean linen, it required that I stalk Bradford Hall while the chambermaids were doing chambermaid stuff. As there was no legitimate reason for me to be in that building unless I was bellhopping on a Sunday, it was very risky. What I had to do was spot a linen storage closet left open while the chambermaid was working in a nearby bedroom. I tiptoed in and took a giant bag of clean linen or towels. Like an overloaded Santa Claus in broad daylight, I would sneak out the back door to my Buick. Sometimes it was a case of toilet paper on my shoulder instead. Tactics in the kitchen at night changed as well, as we now went after cases of staple goods like Kellogg's Corn Flakes as well as cases of perishables like cantaloupe. We got so proficient at obtaining needed items that we began to run out of room to store them in the cottage. As I psychologist now, I think we were all overcompensating after years of deprivation at the hotel. That's where the boat shed came in handy. Since none of us fished, there was plenty of room to stack cartons of toilet paper, cases of dry cereal and bags of linen. The shed had a padlock so all was safe.

Everything was going well at the cottage that summer, until the hotel laundry took linen inventory. A large and inexplicable number of sheets, pillow cases and towels had mysteriously vanished. Once Martin was made aware of the problem, Sherlock Teitelman decided to follow Claude Rain's advice (Casablanca) and "Round up the usual suspects." He made a surprise visit to our cottage late one afternoon in mid-July, during a break between lunch and dinner. Although he had no search warrant, we found ourselves compelled to let him in. Martin insisted on inspecting our closets and cupboards.

He noticed some sheets in the bedroom, towels in the bathroom and dishes in the sink, all belonging to the hotel. He also correctly assumed those were his corn flakes. But in a rare fit of reasonableness, he seemed to recognize that we would be doing just about as much damage if we lived in the Staff House and that he was still taking room and board out of our "salaries." We were ordered to promptly return the soiled linen which was accumulating in our kitchen and were directed not to ever take anything from the hotel again unless we had his prior permission. Wow, it looked like we would get away without serious punishment.

Then Martin decided to take a look outside. He immediately noticed five of the hotel's dozen rowboats on our beach. Hundreds of hotel guests now had seven boats to share, while the five of us had five boats to ourselves. One at a time we had rowed the boats the length of the lake to our cottage. It was not that five of us needed five boats, we just sort of never bothered to return the boats we used. We were instructed to return them immediately.

Having the boats was great. We used them in the afternoon when we got a break between lunch and supper. There had even been an occasion or two in which I talked the other guys into a boat and we rowed to work. Five waiters in tuxedo pants and gold jackets, wearing cummerbunds and black bow ties, in one boat, on a quiet lake, at 6:30 a.m., rowing to work. The fishermen looked on in astonishment as we went by.

But as Martin walked around our little country club and headed down to our private beach, our boat shed caught his eye. Since it was padlocked, it was of even greater interest to him. After a feeble attempt to convince him we had lost the key, we opened the shed. Martin looked as if several major blood vessels supplying his head were about to rupture. He screamed that the five of us had more linen and towels here than the hotel had for 350 guests. Telling him we did not want to run out was not a good idea. Worse yet, some of the stuff we had taken was sitting on the ground in the shed, wet and molding. Boxes of corn flakes were one thing, cases of corn flakes were quite another. It all had to be returned to the hotel that day. We were assured we would all be fired on the next occasion. I knew this was not the end of our trouble. It was not like Martin to let us off with just a hemorrhage.

We knew that Martin could not fire us for what he found at our cottage. We made up too large a proportion of his senior staff, the hotel was busy, and we could not be readily replaced in the middle of the summer, unless Hank could get a few of the local farm boys excused from summer school. Instead, he did what every good executive does when he is unhappy with the conduct of his staff, he made us suffer. Martin claimed to know a great deal about hotel management, but I never believed those schools advertising on match books taught you a whole lot. What was clear, however, was that Martin's major had been hotel management through punishment.

Sometimes it seemed like Martin looked for an excuse to punish the waiters and busboys. There was often labor that the hotel needed to have done and the Teitelman's were too cheap to hire someone to do it. They could make us do it as punishment. Connecticut's labor laws would never get in the way. The most frequent punishment assignments were having to scrub down all of the hundreds of chairs in the dining room or having to dust all of the Venetian blinds. The chairs in the dining room were wooden, with green vinyl seats. The wood frames of the chairs were a natural wood color, and the bottoms were constructed of 1"X1" hardwood stretchers. From the combination of constant use, dust and flying food, the wooden parts would get dirty. Scrubbing the chairs involved sitting on the floor and actually washing each and every visible wooden area on each of the hundreds of chairs. Since one entire wall of the dining room was windows, dusting the Venetian blinds was nothing to sneeze at either.

We had played right into Martin's hands. The chairs were dirty, the blinds were dusty and we were guilty. I always wondered if Martin purposely waited until the dining room needed work, before he dropped in to inspect our cottage. Maybe he did learn something in the match book school. Nevertheless, the cleaning assignment took four days to complete. The only time available for such an undertaking was between lunch and supper, when the dining room was empty. So for most of a week, our precious time off each afternoon was spent cleaning the dining room. The punishment did not stop our borrowing necessities, however. It simply reduced the quantities we took and caused us to regress a bit in the direction of using the trunks of our cars for storage. In hindsight, it was too bad Martin's bookie problem did not occur until a few weeks after his inspection of our cottage. The financial arrangement he and I made weeks later might have granted me immunity from punishment for what we did at the cottage.

There was an occasion later in the summer, however, when obtaining a desired food item from the hotel brought me even closer to the brink of disaster, despite having loaned Martin money. For the reader who might be unfamiliar with the particular food product involved here, a bit of description is in order.

One of the foods consumed in large quantity at the hotel was something called lox. I do not know who named it lox, or why the word is the same in both the singular and plural form, but some people know it as smoked salmon.

Cut into thin strips, this orange-colored, salty, greasy, sometimes fibrous cold fish is extremely expensive. Usually eaten on bagels with cream cheese, it's a favorite of Jewish people. It's one of those odd ethnic foods that you like only if you were raised on it. Everyone else refuses to eat it except people in Iceland and Scandinavia. They live on salmon. A less salty version called Nova Scotia lox, or "Nova" is also available and is even more expensive. Some places sell this stuff for between one and two dollars per slice and you need at least a few slices to adequately endow a bagel. Lox can also be diced, fried and mixed into scrambled eggs or used within an omelet accompanied by sautéed onions. The hotel went through a lot of this stuff. While a Jewish hotel could never run out of lox, it could be stingy with the stuff because of its great cost.

Just because I now had the privilege of eating guest food providing I was discreet and what I ate was reasonable, that did not mean I had legal access to the expensive stuff or the right to eat whatever I wanted whenever I wanted it. But late one hungry evening, I snuck out of Gigolo Duty because I found myself overtaken by an uncontrollable desire to eat some lox. Martin had not been around that evening and the night watchman would petty much ignore me, assuming incorrectly that I was officially serving guests tea and cookies. I sliced three bagels and stuffed them into my pockets. I took a butter knife and some waxed paper with me and entered the walk-in dairy refrigerator, closing the door behind me. In addition to making myself three bagels with cream cheese and lox to go, I stood there and ate slices of lox from the stainless steel pan it was stored in. I ate quite a lot of it. In fact, there was not a whole lot left when I left. Knowing that missing wax paper in the panty was evidence of a crime, I put the wax paper back over the pan as neatly as I could so that my activity might go unnoticed. Returning to the Social Hall, I gave one of the other waiters a bagel. Later, I gave away another bagel, since I was too full to eat it.

The following morning was a breakfast like any other. A bit on the hectic side but nothing seriously out of the ordinary. I did have a lot of people order Postum that morning. I never tried the stuff myself, but it didn't look a lot more palatable than hot prune juice. It was after the meal that trouble began. At about 10:05 a.m., the moment the last guest left, Martin locked the dining room doors and announced loudly that we were to put all livestock away immediately, then promptly stop whatever else we doing and come to the front of the dining room and take a seat. Now this kind of thing had happened before and I knew from experience it was not going to be a board meeting of company executives. Whenever he locked the doors, it meant Martin was very angry about something that happened but did not know who he should be angry at. At the front of the dining room, Martin sat down at the maître d's desk and had us sit down at the tables all around him. The maître d' and captain sat beside him and remained quiet.

Looking almost crazed, Martin began his interrogation of the staff. "Who stole the lox from the kitchen last night?" He repeated the question several more times, getting more angry each time. He made a point of making eye contact with each of the 26 or so staff and kept repeating the question. "Who stole the lox from the kitchen last night?" "No one is going to leave here until I find out who stole the lox last night." I was scared. This time I thought I would be fired. My financial dealings with Martin were not enough. He was not the type to be grateful. Plus he was too angry to be reasonable and the theft was now too public an event. Martin would have to make an example of someone and I knew he could not back down in front of all his employees after all this yelling. How would I get the money back, I wondered, if I no longer worked here. What a disaster. Again he demanded to know "Who stole the lox from the kitchen last night?" I couldn't take much more of this. Guilt was getting to me. I knew that if I did not confess, I would doom all waiters and busboys to days of dark afternoons cleaning the dining room again. Some of these guys were my friends. Although two people knew that I made bagels and lox last night, no one knew about the quantity I ate while inside the refrigerator. Evidently I had eaten too much. Maybe he'd just make me pay for the food but not fire me. For a fleeting instant I thought of Kirk Douglas. If I stood up and said "I'm Spartacus," would the other waiters do the same? Every waiter and busboy claiming *he* was the one who stole the lox. But then Martin hollered again and I returned to reality. "Who stole the lox from the kitchen last night?" At that moment, feeling intense emotional pressure, I decided to confess. But just as I took the breath in, Martin shouted "Every padlock is missing from every refrigerator door and cupboard! Who stole the locks from the kitchen last night?"

It seemed that some employee even more ambitious than me had decided that the best way to assure easy access to hotel food was to disable the hotel's anti-theft system. He had somehow lifted every padlock from the refrigerators and cupboards, probably while they hung unlocked during the Tea Room. Here I was, a millisecond away from confessing to the wrong crime. I now remained quiet, trembling, but quiet. No one confessed and so I spent many afternoons working side by side with my friends, making the dining room into the cleanest fucking place I had ever seen. Meanwhile, the Teitelmans went to the hardware store for replacement padlocks.

Eating lox, borrowing boats, sheets, towels and corn flakes were not the only things we did that cost the hotel money. The busboys in particular never got along well with the hotel's central vacuum cleaning system. Since the entire dining room had to be vacuumed between meals, the hotel had abandoned the use of individual vacuum cleaners. Canister vacuums had resulted in busboys standing around waiting for their turn to use one and they were expensive to repair or replace. So one winter Martin had a central vacuuming system installed. The main unit was in the basement below the dining room and there were outlets to plug a hose into at almost every waiter's station. But the Teitelmans saved money by not buying too many hoses. Now, the busboys waited their turn to use the hoses. Busboys will be busboys and immediately new applications of the central vacuuming system began to appear that the manufacturer had never anticipated.

At the end of each meal, the waiter and busboy had to return all livestock and take all dirty dishes, glasses and silverware to the kitchen. They also had to clean the ashtrays, refill the salt and pepper shakers, refill the sugar bowl, remove the tablecloth and return it and all linen napkins to the linen room. The busboy had to empty the water pitchers, which often meant carrying three or four heavy containers of water all the way to the back of the kitchen just to dump them. Sometimes they dumped the water out a side door of the dining room and onto the lawn, if no one was looking. This was officially prohibited, as it lacked class if hotel guests spotted it being done. Then the busboys wiped down all of the chairs to remove crumbs. And of course they vacuumed.

One of the times Martin locked the dining room doors and called us all down front right after breakfast involved the third costly repair problem with the vacuum system in as many weeks. It seemed that unusual things were appearing in the vacuum's filter, along with the dust and the crumbs it was intended to pick up. Unlike two weeks ago, it was not food in the central vacuum causing the problem. Through repeated experience, learning perhaps, the vacuum had gotten better at handling large chunks of meat. Last week, some busboy avoiding an extra trip to the kitchen with a few items found on the floor that he had missed earlier, vacuumed up three forks and four linen napkins. This time it was something else that the vacuum was not equipped to handle. But Martin was even more disturbed because the vacuum was now more extensively damaged. Someone had vacuumed up a pitcher of water rather than empty it down a sink. Once again, no confession was forthcoming and so by the end of the week the dining room was very clean again. Fortunately for me, this time it was only the busboys who were assigned.

Proving once again the futility of punishment was an event that happened the following Saturday night. At about ten minutes before the dining room opened at 7:00 p.m. for dinner, all of the waiters were carrying out long, rectangular trays full of individual shiny metal cups of fruit cocktail. These were set out just moments in advance of the meal at each guest's place setting. The plan was to serve it cold. Each waiter dished out his own fruit cocktail in the kitchen from the two-gallon cans into the little fruit cups. It was usually a mess in the kitchen. Thirty-four fruit cups would fit on a tray if they were pushed together tightly, side by side. We would use a giant ladle to transfer fruit cocktail from the big cold cans to the little cups.

Regardless of how many cups a waiter needed, he'd position the cups close together so there was little need to fill each one individually and carefully. Rather, they were filled continuously from the ladle. While this method was faster, it also resulted in a lot of fruit cocktail and juice landing on the tray between the individual cups. Gradually, the tributaries of fruit juice would form larger streams and the streams formed rivers. The trays had a small lip around the perimeter, but as a dam it could not stop a raging river of fruit juice. It was not uncommon to see a slightly intoxicated waiter carrying a loaded tray of fruit cocktail from the kitchen on Saturday night, with fruit juice pouring off the back of the tray onto his jacket, pants, the backs of his shoes and the dining room rug. It was just that Saturday night after our scolding about misuse of the vacuum cleaning system, that one of the waiters, Steve Dolinsky, lost a full tray of fruit cocktail.

Now Dolinsky was one who did not carry a tray well to begin with. He was tall and lanky and rather than stay steady, level and balanced, his tray as he carried it always looked like a small boat on a rough ocean. But this night, overloaded with fruit and alcohol, Steve apparently slipped on the fruit juice impregnated carpet created by the waiter that preceded him dripping down the dining room. When Steve fell, no less than the entire contents of 34 cups of fruit cocktail were laying on the carpet. There were thousands of little squares of fruit everywhere. It was five minutes before post time and there was a crowd pushing, trying to escape from the hamster tubes and into the dining room. There was only one solution, and every busboy knew it. The vacuum repairman was back within the week.

Another season was over and now I had some status. The following summer would be my third year as a waiter. I would have a station along the window toward the front of the dining room and have something to say about which busboy was assigned to me. I should be making serious money continually and I expected Martin to remain grateful. The increased income would provide me with more tuition money, more money for my Buick as well as the ability to live off grounds again for the summer. So I decided I'd probably come back.

13
CAPTAIN OF THE WAITERS

When I returned in June for my fourth summer, my third as a waiter, I could not find an available cottage to rent. I was sorry I had not taken John Breslow, the realtor, up on the offer he made me at the end of last summer. When I gave him back the keys to our lakeside villa last September and thanked him for renting it to us, he was pleasantly surprised that it was still in good condition. From our conversation, he could tell how much I liked the place, especially eating corn flakes on the porch in a rocking chair and looking out over the lake. He told me that the cottage was actually for sale now. I could buy it for $4,000. A small, two-bedroom cottage with a porch on a corner lot with a boathouse and its own beachfront for $4,000. Wow. I could own it forever and spend summers here someday. Or I could have John rent it out for me, just not to waiters and busboys. My family could summer here. Then reality hit. I remembered how angry my mother was when I bought a car at age 16 for $15. When I bought another Buick for $20 a year later just for parts (it had a new battery, a rebuilt generator and a new water pump all worth more than the $20 I paid) she was again very unhappy with me. Even explaining that I was simply going to remove the valuable parts and that a junk dealer had already agreed to take the second car from me at no cost, did not calm things in our house. I could only begin to imagine coming home after a summer at the hotel and announcing that instead of having $2,000 available to contribute to my NYU tuition, I bought a cottage. Not even knowing if Connecticut law would allow someone under 21 to enter into a contract to purchase real estate, I had decided that it was too early in my career for cottage ownership. With no cottages available for rent this summer, I ended up renting a small apartment adjacent to the Stanbury Bakery.

The regionally famous Stanbury Bakery was owned by Marek Zaslavski. Marek was in his early 60s, short and slightly heavy, with a strong Eastern European accent and a couple of gold teeth. He supplied all of the bread to the hotel and I once heard a rumor that he was a silent partner in the place. Knowing I was looking for a place to live, Morris T. told me that Marek had a small furnished apartment that adjoined the bakery that might be for rent. I went into town and found Marek in the bakery. He showed me the apartment, which still had someone living there. It had a bedroom, a tiny living room/entry hall, a bathroom and a kitchenette. The price was fair. He offered to rent it to me as of next week when the current tenant moved out. It was a pretty good deal, even closer to the hotel than the rooming house I had lived in two summers earlier and right next to the bakery. Plus, I had privacy. Not a cottage on a lake, but quite acceptable. Free food was possible since it adjoined the bakery. Only after I moved in did I meet the previous tenant. It was Marek's 90-year-old mother. He had moved her out so he could rent to me. I did not know where he moved her to. I did not ask. It was on the old black-and-white TV he left in the room for me that I watched Neil Armstrong and Buzz Aldrin walk on the moon.

The only downside to being in Stanbury again was the back road from Stanbury to the hotel. The road was narrow, full of bad curves, blind hills and an occasional dog. I used to fly down that road. With less than an hour off between breakfast and lunch if we were lucky, driving fast was inevitable. Lots of trips each day on that road, about four miles each way. To the hotel in the early morning, to my room in Stanbury after breakfast, back to the hotel for lunch, back to the room after lunch, back to the hotel for dinner, back to Stanbury after dinner and then most nights back to the hotel for Tea Room, Gigolo Duty or girl hunting. Then one more trip back to Stanbury. I knew the road by heart and went much faster than was safe. The speed limit was 30 MPH but I normally did between 45 and 60 MPH. Because the road was narrow, racing up over a blind hill could be dangerous.

The Buick had a pair of very loud horns. Whether it was 6:30 a.m. or midnight, foggy or clear, when flying around a blind curve or up over a blind hill, the Buick's horns were blaring. That saved my life a few times. I was not the only busboy or waiter on that road who was in a hurry. Joe Goldman, the waiter who speculated what his guests wanted to eat instead of taking their orders, was almost fired after he ran Morris and Edna Teitelman off the road in their Lincoln as he sped toward them coming up over a blind hill.

I had new, beautiful looking white wall tires, but they were retreads. If I hit the right bump in the road at just the right speed (around 50 MPH) the Buick would begin to shake, all over. The steering column would come alive. It was moving up and down while the steering wheel shook left to right. It was as if the Buick was having a grand mal seizure. Just the right speed and the right bump. I believe the physicists refer to this as the "natural period of vibration." In any event, until I could slow the car down dramatically, it was almost out of control. This happened often while flying low on the Stanbury Road.

Lenny's Texaco Station in Stanbury had the solution to my shaking problem. He had a type of tire balancing machine that is now extinct. With the front of the car raised off the ground a bit and the wheels left on, he'd remove a hubcap and put a contraption on that wheel; kind of a helmet made of concentric steel rings that mounted where the hubcap belonged. He'd then roll a device powered by a giant electric motor up against the tire. When he turned it on, it would cause the wheel to spin at high speed. You could see the entire car shake as the wheel began to spin faster and faster. While the wheel was spinning rapidly, he'd touch an adjustment control on the helmet device to change its settings until the car stopped shaking while the wheel spun. Then he'd stop the spinning wheel and read the setting on the helmet. It told him where on the wheel to bang on balance weights and how much. Once that was done on both front tires, the Buick no longer shook. I could now go even faster over blind hills and around bad curves on the Stanbury Road. Another great reallocation of my tuition money.

While my automotive knowledge and skills helped me become a waiter and saved my life in the Chevy wagon, they also resulted in frequent requests from other waiters and busboys to help them with their car problems. One of them, a big guy named Bob Schantz, had a '59 Buick. Bob was so big that more than once he was seen carrying his waiter, my once roommate, the little Louie Sternberg, on top of a waiter's tray upon Bob's shoulder. Being very partial to Buicks and friendly with Bob, I agreed to help him. His radiator was leaking and had to come out. While under his car, I opened a steel line that sent transmission fluid forward to a cooling tank at the bottom of the radiator. His '59 was different from my '55 and I did not realize what was going to happen. My head got covered with transmission oil. I mean covered. I had to use laundry soap to get all of the dirty red oil out of my hair. Repeated shampoos didn't do it. Years later my hair began to thin and recede a bit. To this day I blame Schantz's Buick.

Money for the Buick and my apartment was more readily available this summer, because Martin had surprised me when I arrived by promoting me to captain of the waiters. I was both pretty senior and a good waiter, as well as the guy who bailed his ass out last year, but I was not the only experienced waiter who returned for another summer. When he announced I was captain, I hoped this was not the beginning of a replay of the financial dealings of last year. Car repair, tailoring and gazebo maintenance were the limits of what I was willing to do above and beyond the call of duty this year. I had no intention of getting involved with the banking industry again. Fortunately, Martin was not in need of that assistance this summer.

Being captain of the waiters was an interesting position to be put in. I was now technically the supervisor of all of the other waiters and busboys, many of whom were my friends. But being captain had some very distinct privileges. For one, you were officially able to eat guest food. In fact on rare occasions you could even be seated at the Teitelman table after a meal, joining members of the family, and the maître d'. Not that I would ever want to. You could actually eat real food in public. I already had been granted the privilege of eating guest food as a result of my financial dealings with Martin the previous year, but I was expected to be discreet as there was no official reason or justification for me to be eating food intended for humans. I assumed last year the other boys just thought I had guts and was lucky Martin never caught me. As captain now, while I was still not supposed to flaunt the fact that I was eating human food and was still absolutely prohibited from being seen eating in front of any of the guests during their meal, I now had a known, official entitlement. I had formally risen above the possibility of being fired for eating guest food or needing permission from the chef or the baker as an explanation for doing so. Nor did I have to negotiate for it as I did last year. But while my privilege to eat guest food expanded, my selections became increasingly limited. The hotel was already on the way toward helping me become a vegetarian later in life. Long after I gagged at meatloaf and learned to hold my breath when near boiled beef flanken, common things happened at the hotel that made me sick to my stomach.

The notion of ground up animal livers as a human food item had begun to horrify me. No imagination could match watching chopped liver being made for hundreds of guests. Crates of calves' livers fed one by one through a grinder. The site was bad enough, but the kitchen was hot and the smell was awful. Why were we eating cows? I began to ask myself. Then there was the evening that Martin tossed me keys to the very deep freezer down below the kitchen. It was accessed only by first walking through a large refrigerator in the butcher shop. He sent me down to get a five gallon container of sherbet so that it could be served later, after it warmed up enough to get a scoop into it.

The refrigerator I had to pass through was actually a meat locker. Halves and quarters of steers were hanging from hooks with blood on the floor below them. I kept saying "Excuse me" as I wiggled between them, trying not to touch one as I worked my way to the back and into the deep freezer for sherbet. When Martin had sent me for the sherbet I was just about to begin eating dinner - roast white meat chicken, mashed potatoes and carrots. When I came back up with the sherbet and returned to my dinner, I took a serious look at it. I then went into the kitchen, dumped my entire meal in the trash and made myself two ketchup on rye bread sandwiches. Again I found a sealed bottle of Heinz and took bread from a bag that had never been opened. Despite my privilege to eat guest food in the open, I lost weight at the hotel again that summer.

The other privilege accorded me as the captain was that of not having to do all of the work that all of the other waiters had to do. In the normal division of labor between waiter and busboys, certain duties regularly belong to the busboys and others regularly belong to the waiter. But as captain of the waiters, I did not need to help my busboy in any way, either with setup or cleanup after a meal. Other busboys were assigned to assist my busboy in doing my waiter work. Those busboys were designated as having a side job called "Captain's Station." So as the captain, I basically could stroll into a fully set up station in the dining room when my guests arrived, serve them, and then stroll back out. The entire mess would be cleaned up by my busboy and other busboys assigned to help him, even though they had their own work to do with their own waiter. I could then sit and leisurely enjoy my ketchup on rye sandwiches.

Another luxury I had as captain had to do with the interaction between the waiters in the kitchen. We know guests would get grumpy if they felt the service to be slow or saw others who came in at the same time getting served ahead of them. There could be 12 or more waiters in the dining room taking orders from their guests most of whom came in all at once when the dining room opened. They all rushed to take the orders, get into the kitchen and get on line. If you ended up 10th or 12th on line you would clearly be serving your guests long after other guests had been served. So there was a lot of competition between the waiters trying to get into the kitchen quickly. As captain however, I did not have to participate in the competition. I could take orders from my guests in a more leisurely way and be more apt to get the orders right. I could take time to be friendly and chat with them in an effort to improve my tips. The reason I could take my time was that I did not have to wait on line in the kitchen. Even if the line in the kitchen was already 12 waiters long, when the captain waltzed in, he had the right to "cut" the line. That meant I could go right to the front of the line any time I wished and that was okay with the chefs. The other waiters had no standing to complain. In fact, they would not dare complain, since I was partly responsible for their table and guest assignments each Sunday as well as their busboy and his side job assignments. I also had some authority to fire.

So all in all, as captain of the dining room I was quite a privileged character. It also gave me the absolute right to pick my busboy. I picked a fellow named Jerry Bilstein, who was both a really good guy and a very good busboy. He and I worked very well together that summer. As captain, I had the opportunity to sit with the maître d' on Sunday afternoons when this past week's guests were leaving and new ones were arriving and participate in the table assignments for the incoming guests. I got to see what we knew about incoming guests either as good tippers or bad tippers. I got to see the slips Mrs. Teitelman sent down describing them. Getting to pick my own guests guaranteed I would make serious money and have a reasonably good life that summer at the Teitelman's Inn. So would Jerry. I had risen from low scrotum on the totem to captain. At age 20, making $400 or more per week in 1969 was amazing.

Having more free time as the captain, since others were assigned to do most of my work, I often visited the front desk on Sundays. I wasn't bellhopping now, but rather taking the opportunity to check out a young lady named Ellie Friedman who worked as the secretary, telephone operator and hotel clerk as required. I liked Ellie for three reasons. The first reason was that she would inform me which wealthy guests were due at the hotel in weeks to come. That gave me a head start planning which guests I would ask for when I dealt with Martin and the maître d' at check-in time on Sunday. The other two reasons I liked Ellie stared right at me.

One of Ellie's job duties was to type up and mimeograph the menu, a new one for each meal. Generally two menus were placed in the center of each table for the guests to share. Eight menus per table might have lessened the difficulty waiters had with their guests making up their minds, but paper and mimeograph ink were expensive and so Mrs. T. only provided two to a table per meal. The left side of each lunch menu had a column in which any hotel activities that day would be announced, whether at night in the Social Hall or in the afternoon on the lakefront. For instance, if the hotel's giant, 15-seat paddle boat, known as the "Lake Cruiser" was leaving on a tour of Lake Gilmer at 2:15 today, Ellie published it on the menu. If the hotel's own world-renowned MC, singer and comedian, Mr. Ralph Darling, or any of the fair to middling singers, comedians, or tired vaudeville acts the Teitelmans brought in was appearing in the Social Hall that night at 10:00 p.m., Ellie put it on the menu.

Her brief descriptions of Lake Gilmer on the menu always made me laugh; "peaceful," maybe, but "gorgeous" and "magnificent" were a bit over the top. One day I got Ellie into serious trouble with Mrs. Teitelman, when I convinced her to announce a voyage of the Lake Cruiser on "beautiful, exotic Lake Gilmer." Mrs. T. saw nothing at all "exotic" about the lake. She had obviously never been to our cottage at night.

Ellie's father owned a giant farm in Stanbury. This part of Connecticut had plenty of chickens, chicken coops, cows and cow barns. Some of the dark, secluded places Ellie and I found to go parking stunk horribly from chicken shit when the wind blew the wrong way. Despite popular belief, even teenage boys can be turned off. I was familiar with the smell of dog shit on the sidewalks of New York. Chicken shit was a terrible new experience and having taken my first psychology courses in college and knowing about Pavlov, I worried that the repeated association of sex and the smell of chicken shit was going to somehow cause me psychological harm. In the same way that dogs learned to salivate to a bell paired with food and some people are stimulated to urinate by the sound of running water, perhaps I would inadvertently learn to be aroused by the smell of chicken shit. In technical terms, I could develop a fetish for it. Or later in life, sex would remind me of chickens. I did not want that to happen and so I faced a couple of big choices each time I went parking with Ellie.

The summer went well and I made serious money. I got along well with the staff and never again got a hard time from Martin.

14
BORSCHT TO SPUMONI

After one summer as a busboy, two as a waiter and one as captain, I had one more summer to work before leaving New York for graduate school in Ohio. The hotel had already taught me so many important lessons in life. First, I learned how hard one had to work to make serious money and that ambition and perseverance can pay off. You had to hustle to make a living. I learned that you didn't have to be Jewish to cook Jewish food. You didn't have to speak Yiddish or even English. You could be Chinese. I learned that the preparation of dead animals for consumption as food for humans was disgusting. People eating meat began to look to me as if they were aliens from another planet. I now understood the banking industry, at least some of the illegal aspects, much more clearly and saw the hole gambling can get one into. I learned to virtually run while carrying five hot cups (and saucers) of coffee. I could carry four or five hot main dish plates full of food "butterflied" between my fingers and up my arm without dropping any or getting food from one plate onto the underside of another. I can still do that today and occasionally use the skill to serve or clear an entire table in one operation at a meal for a large family gathering, while the hostess looks on in horror and fear for her fancy china. I learned the power of "prumes." My high speed driving skills on blind hills and turns had greatly improved. I learned how one could evade the requirements of auto registration and auto insurance. My knowledge of human reproductive biology had advanced considerably. I learned patience when dealing with cranky people and honed my bullshitting skills so as to increase my income. My skills advanced at manipulating human behavior, whether it was becoming a waiter and working my way up the corporate ladder, training paying guests to order their food as I directed them to, controlling a dining room full of children or managing a dining room full of teenagers as their captain. I learned how to write a contract that held up and learned great skepticism and fear surrounding the cleanliness of food being served whenever I went out to eat. Clearly, if one's mother did not cook the food herself, it might not be safe to eat.

While the hotel had turned me into Robin Hood (we never viewed it as stealing, but rather taking from the rich and giving to the poor), it had made me almost a vegetarian. Robin Hood the vegetarian. It had also occurred to me that between the chefs with their meat cleavers and Martin's gambling and banking, the adults we worked with may not have had as much sense as we teenagers did.

But beyond the philosophical lessons was the one of greatest importance, I learned to count money, lots of money. Being the first serious money I ever earned, I would arrange it into piles of like bills on my bed. In my early days at the hotel, counting my tips when the guests left on Sunday produced stacks of mainly one dollar bills, some fives and tens. As captain, I usually had a couple of fifties and multiple piles of twenties. Besides my contribution to tuition at NYU, the money kept my $15 Buick on the road for years and restored its beauty, at least in my eyes.

Parting with the hard-earned money taught another of life's lessons. At the end of the summer of 1969 I purchased the first 'transistorized' open-reel tape recorder, so I could record and save for posterity the Doo Wop music I loved. Made by a Japanese company called TEAC, it was among the first such recording devices available that used transistors instead of vacuum tubes. It was built into a beautiful teak wood enclosure. It cost $400 in 1969. A lot of money for those days and especially for a 20-year-old. Handing the store clerk the cash I had worked so hard for was the first time I recall facing so difficult a decision. Did I really want the TEAC? Did I really need it? Was it worth all of that work? Well, I still have it and it still works. It sits on display in a big bookcase in my office.

While I learned many of life's lessons at the hotel, I had more academics to learn. I needed a ninth semester at NYU because I had changed majors twice: first French, then American History and now Psychology. I needed more time to complete the required courses as a psychology major. That meant graduating in January rather than the previous June and that I could not start graduate school until September. One more summer at the hotel? The Teitelmans wanted me back and I knew I could make serious money again.

Unlike previous years, I had not been at the hotel for any of the off-season holidays, except the Jewish Holidays in late September. When I said goodbye to Mrs. Teitelman after that holiday, she asked if I was coming back next summer. I told her I probably would, and it would be the last summer before I left for graduate school. But there was one possible problem I presented to her. I had decided to grow a moustache. The hotel always had a hard and fast rule of no facial hair. Somewhat longer hair, though not hippy length, was being tolerated because almost all the boys had it. But not facial hair. I told Mrs. T. that if I came back next summer it would be with a moustache. She said that was fine as long as it was well-groomed. Obviously, she was accepting of moustaches. Mr. T. looked like Groucho.

In early May I called Martin and told him I'd be returning in mid-June. He seemed pleased. When I arrived, I planned to stay with my aunt and uncle in Plain Ridge until I found a nice place or organized a group of us to rent a cottage if possible, as I had done two years before. The afternoon I walked into the dining room,

Martin was at the Family Table, sitting with a couple of people I did not know. Instead of greeting me, since I was the guy who was his captain last year and who had kept him from sleeping with the fish the summer before, he just looked at me and in his loud, dumb voice said, "You're not working with that moustache." I fired back "I'm not working without it." I had grown a nice, full moustache of the Fu Manchu variety. Martin repeated his proclamation and I in turn told him he might want to talk to his mother. I explained that I had discussed the matter with her last September before I left and she was fine with it. I was not going to be working without it. Usually, once Martin was backed into a corner in public he would never be reasonable. But Martin backed down, which really surprised me. And in front of people. Okay.

Once we got past the moustache issue, I asked which staff were back so I could begin setting up teams of waiters and busboys. I assumed I was still the captain. Martin informed me otherwise and it was not because of the moustache. I had not been at the hotel for any of the holiday weekends since September or during Passover in April. Martin had struggled for staff as he usually did in the off-season and had promoted Jerome Bilstein to captain.

I knew Jerry well. He had been my busboy the previous summer when I was captain. Jerry had a lot of experience at the hotel in previous years and since he lived close to the hotel, he worked on all of the holiday weekends that the hotel was open. He had worked as a busboy when needed and worked as a waiter when needed during the off-season. He was a really good guy and a very good busboy or waiter. The previous year when I was captain, Jerry was very willing to be the captain's busboy rather than take on the role of a waiter because he knew he could make as much money as the captain's busboy as he would make as a waiter and knew that there would be other busboys assigned to help him. Plus, he saw the busboy role as one of a lot less grief. Jerry and I had a good summer working together last year and I liked to think I had been a good boss. When Martin told me that Jerry had been captain through the entire off-season and he did not want to demote him, I was okay with that. Jerry becoming my boss did not concern me. I knew there were usually enough B and B+ guests to go around.

My respect for Jerry turned out to be reciprocated. When he arrived later that afternoon and spoke with me, he took it upon himself to tell Martin that captain or not, he was not taking the station in the dining room that was traditionally the captain's station. He would instead take the next station up along the window. He wanted me to work from the captain's location even if he was the captain. Initially Martin objected, but soon gave in. Clearly Jerry was not just a good guy; he remembered who looked out for him and he was loyal.

It made me feel really good.

I headed for my aunt and uncle's house that night and was back at the dining room working the next afternoon as we set up for our first guests, tonight. Once again, I was in tuxedo pants, black shoes and socks, a white shirt, bow tie, cummerbund, gold waiter's jacket and sporting my gold waiter's buttons. I still have the buttons. Although I was not captain, I got to pick my busboy and influence which guests were assigned to me. Jerry got first choice, but then made certain I would be pleased with my guests, many of whom we had served together the previous summer. I was working from the captain's station along the windows.

After that meal was over and the guests left, Martin spotted me sitting in the far corner of the dining room alone, eating "guest" food. Normally the staff ate before the guests. The chef, still assuming I was a big shot, gave me what I asked for - potatoes and vegetables. I took fruit salad and lots of pastry. I wasn't flaunting it, but I wasn't hiding either. As captain last year, I had the "privilege" of eating guest food and as Martin's financial savior the year before, guest food was part of the deal. I was going to continue eating guest food and I was not going to hide near the pot washers or risk death by taking food down whole and choking. I also assumed some level of loyalty on

Martin's part. How naïve I was.

Martin approached me and explained that I did not have the right to eat guest food this year, as I was not the captain. He was smart enough not to get into this argument with me in front of everyone. He did his best to whisper considering that in addition to mutations in his laugh gene, his whisper chromosome had damage as well. I told him to take a hike. Over the next few days, similar interactions with Martin were repeated. I just ignored him when he told me to stop eating guest food as I continued to do it anyway. I was not eating anything costly to the hotel. Meat was virtually gone from my diet. I wasn't sure if for Martin this was a matter of principle, fear of precedent or just chest thumping between pant-hoots. Most likely the latter. Plus, he was still giving me shit about my moustache.

I had not yet begun looking for a place to live for the summer, as I was welcome at my aunt and uncle. Martin was getting me angry. I'd come too far at this place and done too much for him to be treated this way. Sunday after we served lunch (dinner as the hotel called it), after I received my tips and all of the guests had left, I announced that I quit. Martin looked shocked, but never said a word. I suspect his only concern was for his gazebo. I said goodbye to Jerry and some of the other waiters and busboys and then promptly left the dining room. I stopped briefly at the

Main House to say goodbye to Mrs. T. and tell her why I was leaving. She tried to talk me out of it and said she would speak to Martin. I thanked her but said no and headed for my aunt's house to get some sleep, collect my clothes and say goodbye. I drove back to New York early the next morning. Another of life's lessons learned. I had principles. I was not for sale and neither was my moustache.

I still needed a job that summer. I had worked at a Buick dealer in Westchester as a mechanic for a time in the early spring after my extra semester ended and I received my degree. But I wasn't really cut out for that. I knew a lot, but not enough. I decided to look for another waiter job, as I was now quite experienced.

I found a position at a restaurant in White Plains, New York. It was a small Italian restaurant, a very Italian restaurant called Luciano's, serving regional Italian cuisine. I'm still not sure exactly what that means. The restaurant was family owned and run and not affiliated with any restaurants with the same name. Luciano was the oldest of the three brothers, all of whom worked there. The middle brother, Lorenzo, tended bar. The maître d' was Renaldo. I was one of only four waiters. The walls were decorated with autographed photos of famous Italians and many of the chairs had brass plaques on the back commemorating the famous Italian who once sat there. I could not find Frank

Sinatra anywhere, but I often had the privilege of dusting crumbs off the chair that Sergio Franchi once sat in. The restaurant had been written up in New York's Cue magazine. It was romantic and expensive. When the sound system wasn't playing Domenico Modugno singing "Nel blu dipinto di blu" over and over, on Saturday nights Luciano's had entertainment, generally a three piece band – a bass, drums, a piano and a female singer. I often wished I was a patron with his date rather than a waiter. When Enzo the chef had hot food ready sitting under the heat lamps and I did not pick up fast enough, he would lecture me in the kitchen. He would tell me "If you wanta make a money, you got to mova U S."

The restaurant was not chaotic like the hotel. It was small, did not accommodate a large number of people and had a small staff. Saturday nights, it wasn't the waiters who were drunk, it was the owners. Most of the food was good. Unlike the hotel, they fed the staff. I loved the baked stuffed clams. Enzo would even make a fancy meal for management and staff on Saturday afternoons, before we opened for dinner. When he served pig's knuckles, I stayed outside in my '55 Buick to avoid the sight and smell.

Enzo would also make his own bouillon. He'd get cow bones somewhere and wrap them in a tablecloth. The package would then be lowered into a huge pot to which he added boiling water. They were then left to soak for a few days. This further reinforced my vegetarian tendencies. One day the cat that hung around the back door to the kitchen fell into the bouillon. Enzo got him out. The cat spent a week trying to lick himself clean. The cat survived and so did the bouillon. Enzo served the bouillon to the guests.

It was now clear that while I had gone from borscht to spumoni, in so many ways nothing had really changed. That was the summer of Luciano, Lorenzo, Gregorio, Ronaldo, Enzo and Ken, my last summer as a waiter. In early September, the Buick and I left for graduate school in Ohio.

About the Author

K.L. Laytin, Ph.D. is a psychologist practicing in Plymouth, Massachusetts. His specialty is Applied Behavior Analysis with children and adults. For many years, he worked as the Director of Psychological Services at state-run residential facilities for developmentally disabled adults. He continues to consult to families and schools regarding children with challenging behavioral issues.

Although his career as a busboy and waiter was long ago, the experiences have remained vivid to him. Parts of this book were written over the last four decades. He still shows off by carrying four or five hot dishes or five cups of coffee at once when serving friends or family at home. When not reminiscing about his days as a waiter or practicing psychology, Dr. Laytin is a software developer and antique Buick hobbyist. Along with his wife, he has a software business that can be found at www.littleguysoftware.com. Information about his behavioral psychology practice can be found at www.behaviordoc.com. He is an expert on 1954 and 1955 Buick automobiles and volunteers as a technical advisor to the Buick Club of America. His own Buick, a 1954 Roadmaster Convertible was recovered from an Oklahoma junkyard in 1988, restored almost entirely by him, and is a national prize winner. It has appeared on the cover of three national magazines. Completion of "When Good Waiters Do Bad Things" is something he has long wanted to find time for.

A Message to the Reader

Dear Reader,

I have chosen to publish this book myself, through an Amazon company called CreateSpace. Self-publishing allows me full control over the book's appearance, but does not give me the marketing power and ability to promote the book that is available through a traditional publisher.

I am asking for your help. If you enjoyed the book and think that others would enjoy it as well, please visit Amazon.com and locate the book by its title or the ISBN on the back cover. There you can give it a star rating and a brief review, if you wish. Doing so will help others find the book and assist me in marketing.

I hope "When Good Waiters Do Bad Things" made you laugh. Thanks for your help.

KLL

January, 2019

CPSIA information can be obtained
at www.ICGtesting.com
Printed in the USA
BVHW041946140719
553413BV00016BA/269/P